D1084748

# PRESERVING
# FAMILIES

# OTHER RECENT VOLUMES IN THE SAGE FOCUS EDITIONS

# PRESERVING FAMILIES
## Evaluation Resources for Practitioners and Policymakers

Edited by
## Ying-Ying T. Yuan
## Michele Rivest

**SAGE** PUBLICATIONS
*The International Professional Publishers*
Newbury Park   London   New Delhi

*For information address:*

SAGE Publications, Inc.
2111 West Hillcrest Drive
Newbury Park, California 91320

HV
699
P73
1990

SAGE Publications Ltd.
28 Banner Street
London EC1Y 8QE
England

SAGE Publications India Pvt. Ltd.
M-32 Market
Greater Kailash I
New Delhi 110 048 India

Printed in the United States of America

Library of Congress Cataloging-in-Publication Data

Preserving families : evaluation resources for practitioners and policymakers /
   edited by Ying-Ying T. Yuan, Michele Rivest.
       p.   cm. -- (Sage focus editions : v. 117)
    "September, 1989."
    Includes bibliographical references.
    ISBN 0-8039-3685-0. -- ISBN 0-8039-3686-9 (pbk.)
    1. Family services--United States--Evaluation.   2. Human services-
-United States--Evaluation.  I. Yuan, Ying-Ying T.   II. Rivest,
Michele
HV699.E86   1990
362.82'8'0973--dc20
                                   90-32813
                                       CIP

**FIRST PRINTING, 1990**

**Sage Production Editor: Susan McElroy**

# *Contents*

# Foreword

CECELIA E. SUDIA

The recent development and expansion of family preservation programs is an unparalleled phenomenon. Over the past fifteen years, the number of programs has grown from a handful to several hundred, although this still falls far short of the 3,000 that would be needed to ensure that services would be available in each county in the country. The provision of home-based family-centered services to child welfare families is a novel approach and an expensive one, and it is still very far from being established as an expectation for all families at risk of having a child placed in out-of-home care or in need of specialized reunification services to assist the return home of a child already in care.

Administrators and legislators hesitate to make the needed investments of training and staff without convincing evidence that the programs are effective and cost-effective. In addition, current evaluation is frequently very limited and provides an inadequate data base from which to answer the problems asked by administrators and funding agencies. The evaluation resource that this volume represents is much needed at this critical juncture. The Edna McConnell Clark Foundation and the Center for the Support of Children are to be commended for its development, and for their felicitous choice of writers and editors.

Program managers and directors are urged to make use of this resource to document the effectiveness of their programs, using the models and techniques provided. I would particularly like to emphasize the need to develop adequate and convincing cost data. The higher costs of these services, plus the fact that the costs must be amortized over future months, make it critical for programs to be able to provide this information in a clear and convincing manner.

In addition, it is important to provide analysis by problem category. From a family systems point of view, it does not matter whether the problem is child abuse or an out-of-control teenager—child protection agencies need assurance that the programs work for their children, and that developmentally the child is doing well when the service ends, not just that the family is still intact.

I am pleased to have had a role in the planning and review of this evaluation resource, and I am sure that its use will lead to needed development in the field of family preservation and related services.

# Acknowledgments

This book originated as a project developed by the editors under the auspices of the Center for the Support of Children, Washington, D.C. We thank the Center for providing a home for this project and organizing the meeting that stimulated the discussions among the chapter authors. We especially thank Laurene McKillop, director of the Center, for her support of this project, from the very beginning when it was just an idea through the dissemination of the initial publication, titled *Evaluation Resources for Family Preservation Services*, upon which this book is based. Terri Nickel of the Center was invaluable in the preparation of the original manuscript. We are all grateful to her for her skills, humor, and patience in working with all of us. We thank Patty Durso for the preparation of the revised manuscript.

Several experts in the child welfare and mental health fields helped us in the early designing of the resource manual and in sharpening our thinking through their review of early drafts. We thank Philip AuClaire, Frank Farrow, Peter Forsythe, David Haapala, Jane Knitzer, Walter McDonald, Susan Notkin, and Cecelia Sudia for their insights and encouragement. We have learned much from each of them and acknowledge their distinct contributions to bettering the lives of children in this country.

Finally, we extend our appreciation for the support of our initial project to the Edna McConnell Clark Foundation, New York. Peter Forsythe, Vice President of the Clark Foundation, stimulated our early thinking and has continued to challenge us to ask questions and seek solutions that may be useful to practitioners and policy-makers in the field and in turn may assist the children and families served by human service agencies.

Ying-Ying T. Yuan
Michele Rivest

*1*

# Introduction

YING-YING T. YUAN
MICHELE RIVEST

This volume has been written primarily for evaluators and administrators who are involved in analyzing family services. An evaluator may play one or more roles, including reviewer of program accountability, provider of objective data to program managers, information gatherer for policymakers, consultant to consumers and stakeholders, and independent researcher. To assist evaluators and administrators, this book discusses the key issues in family services—with special attention to family preservation services—that policymakers consider when deciding to implement, maintain, or expand such programs. Policy issues are an inherent part of the evaluation process. Given the critical role that policymakers—from state and county agency officials to state and federal legislators—play in requiring program evaluation and establishing state and local family services programs, we present issues of concern that will assist policymakers in their decision-making roles.

We use family preservation services as our primary case example in discussing and evaluating family services throughout this volume. Family preservation services are defined as intensive in-home family-based services that are provided to prevent the removal of one or more children from a family. These services have emerged as one of the most strategic program options for child welfare, mental health, and juvenile justice systems. The early pilot programs reported considerable success both in preventing placement and in cost savings. Consequently, these programs have attracted a great deal of interest from many sectors during the past several years.

Family preservation services have received national and state-level attention for several reasons:

- From a policy perspective, these programs have demonstrated their effectiveness in providing preplacement services and in diverting children from substitute care—core mandates of P.L. 96-272, the Child Welfare and Adoption Assistance Act of 1980.
- From a programmatic perspective, many practitioners are supporting a new service philosophy that emphasizes providing services to the family as a whole rather than focusing on the parents or the child as individuals, each served by different programs.
- From a funding perspective, public and private dollars have provided an impetus for realigning program budgets toward prevention and away from out-of-home placement.
- From a national perspective, several research and demonstration efforts have stimulated the creation of these programs by providing information and technical assistance. Throughout the country, family preservation services are being considered by both public and private providers.

Family preservation programs focus on the goal of strengthening the family's ability to care for its children and thereby prevent unnecessary out-of-home placement. These programs typically share the following set of essential characteristics:

- Services are provided to the family as the client, although specific activities may be undertaken to meet the needs of particular family members.
- Services are targeted to those families at imminent risk of having children placed out of the home.
- Services are intensive, which is achieved through low caseloads of 2-6 families per worker at any given time. In many programs,

caseworkers may provide 15-20 hours of service per week to a family.
- Services are time limited (ranging from four to six weeks to less than six months) and flexible in both location and scheduling, to meet the family's needs.
- Services include a mix of clinical, therapeutic intervention, and concrete assistance involving child care, housing, transportation, and other basic supports.

Given the newness of these programs, the range of service methodologies, and the high interest in promoting and expanding these services, evaluators are increasingly being called upon to provide both program and cost analyses of such programs. As these programs come under greater scrutiny, evaluators are playing a major role in assessing family preservation services and other family services, and are thereby participating in the development and expansion of these programs.

The basic issues presented in this volume are applicable in evaluating a variety of ongoing programs as well as demonstration programs in the human services field. Program features of importance for conducting an evaluation are discussed in depth, including program descriptions, target populations, services, client outcomes, cost analysis, and evaluation design. Together, analyses of these six features ensure a comprehensive analysis of the particular program under consideration for evaluation.

Evaluation is now commonly accepted as a critical part of demonstration services and is seen both as a measurement of effectiveness and as a means of learning more about social services delivery on the whole. Program evaluation is in a critical position to improve and reform the quality of family and child services. Seldom will evaluation be the sole determinant of public policy, but it is an important contributor and can provide a clearer assessment of the efficiency and effectiveness of service options.

This book presumes a basic knowledge of evaluation theory and practice. More specifically, it assumes that the evaluator and program administrator have decided upon the overarching goals of the evaluation and a general approach. Each chapter raises a particular issue pertinent to the design of a comprehensive or special-focus study. We have not undertaken a how-to manual; rather, we have sought to discuss the issues that are related to describing and evaluating programs. We include a lengthy discussion of program description components because many of these components may become variables in understanding the effectiveness of different program models. By understanding a program from the perspectives of families, providers, administrators, and the general public, an evaluator can be more responsive to the many demands that may be put upon him or her. We have tried to keep our comments grounded in the basic everyday experiences of public and private agencies undertaking evaluation activities and in the needs of policymakers and other advocates for children.

Each chapter addresses a critical program issue. In Chapter 2, Leonard Feldman concentrates on issues involved in defining the target population. Clear definition of the target population and explicit, measurable screening criteria are critical to successful program evaluation. The definition of target clients is a strategic decision that affects all elements of a program's design. With the emphasis on preventing out-of-home placement as a primary goal of family preservation programs, target population issues such as what families are at risk of placement, how these assessments are made, who makes these determinations, and what type of referral and acceptance criteria are used are key questions for program evaluators.

Chapter 3, by Kristine E. Nelson, presents a detailed overview of the context of family preservation services and the service delivery structure. It offers guidance to the evaluator on describing these services on many different dimensions, including program history and context and program operations involving service model, staffing, client flow, and accountability.

In Chapter 4, Carol L. Pearson presents and discusses a service delivery taxonomy, various measurement and data collection methods, and options for analyzing service delivery strategies. This chapter assists the evaluator in distinguishing the rich variety of services that family preservation programs provide, from clinical and therapeutic interventions, to concrete services such as child care and transportation, to case management functions.

Chapter 5, by Mark Fraser, discusses program outcomes and methods for capturing the clinical and service goals of the program. This chapter focuses on the impact of family preservation services and provides the evaluator with strategies for measuring change in children, parents, and families as a means of documenting program effectiveness. Further, out-of-home placement, which is a critical outcome measure from the standpoint of public policy, is discussed in its many different facets.

Chapter 6, by Ying-Ying T. Yuan, examines the central issues involved in analyzing service delivery costs. It includes discussion of the issues to be taken into account in comparing costs among different programs and between family preservation programs and alternative programs. There are many complex fiscal issues involved in how to finance these programs—from expanding the use of federal dollars to realigning state budgets by shifting costs from foster care to family preservation—and this chapter informs the evaluator of the intricacies involved in conducting cost analyses of these programs.

Finally, in Chapter 7, Leonard Bickman provides statistical guidelines for the construction of evaluation designs using control groups, for those evaluators who are addressing program impact. The chapter shows how researchers can increase the ability of an evaluation to detect meaningful program effects and how they can attribute these effects more clearly to the operation of the program.

# 2

# *Target Population Definition*

## LEONARD FELDMAN

Clear definition of the target population and explicit, measurable screening criteria are critical to successful program evaluation. The definition of the target clients is a strategic decision that affects the evaluator's ability (a) to determine if the program is reaching the families to which it is addressed, (b) to develop a client typology of families most likely to benefit from the program, and (c) to conduct comparisons with other service approaches. The determination of imminence of risk of placement is a key screening criterion for family preservation programs. Risk assessment should be based on a protocol that measures child, parent, and family behavior and functioning within the context of the family's environment. It is also important to set standards for exclusion of clients the program is not equipped to serve. The quality and consistency of program referrals is affected by such factors as community education, training and designation of screeners, use of protocols, and restriction of referral sources.

One of the most critical aspects of both program design and program evaluation is the definition of the target population to be served by the program and followed in an evaluation. Rossi, Freeman, and Wright (1979) define the target population as "persons, households, organizations, communities, or other identifiable units to which interventions are directed in social programs" (p. 17). To be able to test a program model in a meaningful manner, one must first have a clear idea of the numbers, characteristics, and needs of the clients to be served. The evaluator can use this information in a number of ways: to participate in the development or refinement of the intake screening protocol, to develop a sampling strategy that will allow generalization of the results to the target population, and to develop outcome measures. "The choice of the target population is a strategic decision" (Rossi et al., 1979, p. 75). Careful client definition is an important evaluation issue in a number of areas. It can assist the program evaluator in the following tasks:

- determining whether or not the program is reaching the families to which it is addressed
- developing a client typology—identifying the types of clients thought to be appropriate for the program
- conducting comparisons with other client samples of the program over time
- conducting comparisons with other programs using similar or traditional service approaches

Programs such as family preservation are developed to prevent an identified community problem, out-of-home placement. The number and characteristics of the population targeted to receive services are based on this identified need, the availability of resources, and the intervention model chosen. Other factors such as legal, political, or funding expectations and mandates and other providers in the catchment area also strongly affect decisions about who will be considered service eligible.

Early involvement of the evaluator in the program development cycle is desirable. Consultation about program design can aid in the construction of tightly drawn definitions of the target population and case selection criteria. If the program planners wish or are mandated, for example, to measure the efficacy of a program to prevent the breakup of families with adolescents at risk of imminent placement, an operational or working definition of this risk group can be developed and a catchment area defined to the satisfaction of both the program staff and the evaluator.

Evaluators hired after the program design has been established and not integrally related to the project agency can still aid in tightening up the target population definition and client screening tool. Some form of reliability testing of the screening tool could be conducted.

A number of problems arise when the target population is not carefully defined or when the unit of analysis—family or children—is not clearly specified. Criticisms are often made about the equivocal success of new social programs in meeting the needs of community members. To date, evaluations of family preservation services programs—programs targeted at preventing child placement—have demonstrated only clouded empirical support for improved effectiveness of these interventions over existing services (Barth & Berry, 1987; Magura, 1981). Certain populations may benefit greatly from this model. Other groups or subpopulations may not benefit as much. The evaluations conducted in support of these programs have not succeeded very well in distinguishing the populations most effectively served from those that are not. This can be attributed, in part, to a lack of precise target population definition.

Lack of definition can produce great difficulty for the evaluator in successfully accomplishing the primary evaluation objectives. This can be especially detrimental to the evaluator's attempts to determine whether or not the program is reaching and successfully serving the children and families targeted during program design. The lack of case comparability in defining who is at risk of placement has also hampered comparisons across studies (Jones, 1985; Stein, 1985).

Conflict and friction are not uncommon between evaluators and program staff, even under the best of conditions. Without careful definition of the target population and selection criteria, practitioners, guided by their service role, may want to include families in the program only on the basis of professional intuitive knowledge and experience. Practitioners often make decisions about who is at risk of out-of-home placement in response to learning about difficult family situations. Worker judgment about the need for placement has been shown to be unstandardized, often based on intuition, value judgments, or nonclinical issues or ideologies. Different factors are considered by different workers (Gruber, 1980; Jones, 1985; McDonnell, 1985; Segal & Schwartz, 1985; Stein & Rzepnicki, 1983). Prevention of placement projects with low placement rates at termination, such as Homebuilders in Washington, may not have dealt exclusively with high-risk cases. Kinney (1978) notes, "It has been extremely difficult, however, to make sure that only those clients who are actually at the point of entry into placement are being referred for Homebuilders' treatment" (p. 35). It has also been demonstrated that only a small proportion of children designated as at risk of placement actually enter out-of-home care (Leeds, 1986; Stein, 1985).

Difficulty may also arise in getting enough referrals for the new program. This may be especially so because out-of-home placement is actually a low-probability event. It is a common error to overstate subject availability, especially if the target population is not carefully defined and an assessment of the size of the population is not completed prior to program start-up (Rossi et al., 1979). The pool of available subjects to study is usually further diminished by client refusal to participate at intake and by client dropouts while receiving services (Hargreaves & Attkisson, 1978). The dropout problem may be further exacerbated due to the selection of inappropriate clients by virtue of vague definition of the target population or loose selection criteria. Thus the selection criteria are as important as the definition of the target population. They operationally define the rules for screening clients in or out of the program.

The evaluator, if involved at the earlier stages of program development, can assist in estimating the size of various target population groups. Incidence and prevalence rates can be calculated using existing placement agency and census data. Extant social indicator data such as percentage of population below the poverty line, juvenile delinquency rates, child abuse rates, percentage of the neighborhood population with residency under one year, and substance abuse rates may be helpful in prioritizing implementation sites. Key informant surveys and community meetings can also be used to supplement the more robust methods mentioned above (Rossi et al., 1979). Key informant surveys and community meetings can also have a secondary, salutary effect: These interchanges allow further discussion and refinement of the target population definition before the program begins.

Not only does the target population need to be defined, but a clear set of guidelines must exist to ensure the selection of appropriate clients. Target clients must be explicitly described in measurable terms. Inadequate specification of target participants can lead to an increase in inappropriate referrals, high client attrition, and artificially high or low out-of-home placement rates. Results that seem to indicate program failure may actually be an artifact of failure to address this step carefully in the design phase (Rossi et al., 1979).

## Issues Regarding Target Population Definition for Family Preservation Services

A number of factors affect the definition of the target population:

- philosophy, goals, and models of agency service delivery
- agency policy standards
- program start-up considerations
- expectations and mandates of various stakeholders
- public or private agency status
- geographic catchment
- financial and staff resources of the program

The selection of the intervention model is intimately tied to the characteristics of the target population and vice versa. The program developer may exclude a number of client groups based on characteristics or problems he or she feels would not be amenable to treatment by staff using the program model. For example, since many family preservation interventions are very short term (4 to 6 weeks), severe substance abusers or chronically mentally ill parents are sometimes excluded from these programs. Other client groups often excluded are families in which removal of the children is due to homelessness, chronic multiproblem families that move in and out of crisis, and families unmotivated to participate in the program or have their children remain in the home. Most programs specify that at least one adult in the home must be willing to work toward a goal of preventing placement (Lloyd & Bryce, 1984).

The definition of the target population is also related to state laws, jurisdictional regulations, and policies and standards that define who is at risk of abuse or neglect or out-of-home placement. No matter whom an agency would like to target for assistance, agency policy or statutory limitations create requirements that have to be met for client groups with particular characteristics to receive agency services or be eligible for referral to in-home intensive service programs.

The development of the proposed program and the determination of who is eligible to participate can be viewed as a political task (Rossi et al., 1979; Siegel, Attkisson, & Carson, 1978). External pressures affect target population definition and selection. The political and economic contexts surrounding the planning and funding of an intervention program are major forces. Siegel et al. (1978) note, "All human service programs have a heterogeneous group of stakeholders" (p. 219). The list can include politicians, program funders, agency policymakers, the courts, other community providers, community residents, and service recipients themselves. The funding source naturally has a major voice in defining target client groups. If the child protective services agency is purchasing the home-based services, it is more than likely that protective services clients will be the prime target for intervention.

Elected officials can have both direct and indirect effects on client selection. The legislature in New York State authorized the funding for and shaped the operation of several intensive placement prevention projects (Jones, 1985). Recent legislation in California led to the creation of a number of family preservation projects (Yuan & McDonald, 1987). The California legislature, in authorizing funding, also mandated the level of placement prevention (75%) necessary to embody success.

Program developers and evaluators also need to be sensitive to how their programs and studies are viewed by their communities and to take into account the views expressed by various community members during target population definition and the development of the actual client selection process. "The major point is that communities are not passive, unreactive collectives just waiting for an experiment to take place" (Riecken & Boruch, 1974, p. 181). In one way or another, communities shape programs. In a report on the development of home-based service programs in Maine, Hinckley (1984) notes that it was essential to develop community-based program steering committees that participated in the development of program policies, identification of referral procedures, and the establishment of target population priorities.

Stakeholder expectations and mandates can influence not only the number of clients to be served in a service period, but their characteristics as well. Sometimes this occurs in unintended ways. If a legislature mandates a 65% or 75% "success" or placement prevention rate, it could induce or influence program staff to select clients who are more likely to succeed.

Program start-up also can affect the definition of the target population. Program planning staff may wish to expand the service eligibility criteria gradually. At start-up, the criteria may be more restrictive, allowing the newly formed treatment staff an opportunity to gain experience with "less difficult" clients. One type of restriction is to exclude families with children who have experienced multiple placements. Experience has shown that programs are less successful with children who have a history of out-of-home placement than with children who are at risk of first-time placement (AuClaire & Schwartz, 1986).

During the first few months of program operation of the New Jersey Family Preservation Services Program (Feldman, 1987), a restriction was placed on the frequency and length of time of previous out-of-home placements experienced by children referred to the program. For acceptance into the program, all families had to have children at imminent risk of placement. However, during the first few months of program operation, families with children in a prior placement exceeding 90 days or a history of multiple placements were ineligible for services. As staff gained more proficiency, these eligibility requirements were relaxed.

Public or private agency status also can have an effect on the definition of the target population. A public agency, in fact, may have less latitude in defining the target population because of legal or administrative mandates. Such an agency is usually the agency of last resort. More rigid staffing and caseload requirements may also affect the targeting of services for a public sector agency.

The geographic area covered by a service agency also influences the definition of the target population. Programs developed in rural areas, for example, may need broader definition and selection criteria to compensate for the lower incidence and prevalence rates of the area.

The financial and staff resources of the program also shape target population definition and selection. Within the framework of the fiscal resources, client selection criteria can limit prospective clients to those most in need of the service or to those who appear to have the highest probability of success.

## *Defining the At-Risk Population*

### Populations at Risk

Family preservation services are directed to aiding families with children at risk of out-of-home placement. The determination of risk is based on multiple factors of child, parent, and family behavior and functioning within the context of the community. For example, parent or child problems that could lead to child placement include the following:

- actual abuse and neglect
- serious risk of abuse and neglect
- runaway behavior
- out-of-control child behavior

- poor parent-child relationships
- juvenile delinquency
- domestic violence
- parental incapacitation
- parent or child request for removal
- suicidal behavior

The assessment process must be multidimensional, measuring each factor's contribution to placement risk along a continuum and relative to the availability of social supports, community resources, and the success of past interventions.

Within an ecological framework, the intervention focus is on the relationships among family members and those between family members and their interpersonal environment, a network of family, friends, neighbors, resources, and the primary systems and services in the community (Lloyd & Bryce, 1984). By focusing on the social context in which families live, a framework is provided for considering the interactions between social forces and individual and family characteristics (Spearly & Lauderdale, 1983). High-risk families have been found to be less socially integrated into society. These families are deemed socially isolated and have low levels of support from friends and relatives (Belsky, 1978; Horowitz & Wolock, 1981; Polansky, Ammons, & Gaudin, 1985; Polansky, Gaudin, Ammons, & Davis, 1985).

The parents' social environment has a significant effect on child rearing. It is believed that a fragile family can care adequately for its children given a sufficiently supportive setting (Garbarino & Sherman, 1980). "High-risk families are most likely to live in high-risk neighborhoods both because their personal histories incline them to do so and because the political and economic forces that shape residential patterns encourage them to form clusters" (Garbarino & Sherman, 1980, p. 196). Support for the concept that "high-risk" neighborhoods contribute to child maltreatment is also provided by Spearly and Lauderdale (1983) and Camasso and Wilkinson (in press). Spearly and Lauderdale found that county rates of child abuse were directly related to the proportion of mothers under economic and social stress. The "high-risk" environment is likely to be nonresponsive to the needs of a family at risk. Camasso and Wilkinson demonstrate that in the counties of a mining state with rapidly growing "boomtowns," the rate of child abuse and neglect is far higher than in other counties. These authors believe that boomtown communities may offer decreased neighborliness and increased isolation of families.

Bronfenbrenner (1979) interweaves this ecological framework with the concepts of parental role, life stressors, and social supports to summarize how child-rearing practice is a function of the interplay between a person and his or her environment:

> But whether parents can perform effectively in their child-rearing roles with the family depends on role demands, stresses, and supports emanating from other settings. As we shall see, parents' evaluations of their own capacity to function, as well as their view of their child, are related to such external factors as flexibility of job schedules, adequacy of child care arrangements, the presence of friends and neighbors who can help out in large and small emergencies, the quality of health and social services, and neighborhood safety. The availability of supportive settings is, in turn, a function of their existence and frequency in a given culture or subculture. This frequently can be enhanced by the adoption of public policies and practices that create additional settings and societal roles conducive to family life. (p. 7)

Lack of clarity about the at-risk concept can arise when the screening tool (if one is employed) is used to measure a unitary concept such as risk of abuse and neglect rather than all salient factors mentioned above that affect the safety and well-being of family members. Child members of a family can certainly be at risk of abuse and neglect without being at imminent risk of out-of-home placement. Thus such a family may not be eligible for a family preservation services program.

**Defining the Risk of Out-of-Home Placement**

The evaluator can help bring clarity to this crucial task by contributing to the process, factors, and tools used in the determination of the risk of out-of-home placement. The methods used to select and screen families will affect decisions about the evaluation goals, outcome criteria, and validation of the model for clients with specified characteristics.

A number of researchers have developed risk assessment tools or guidelines for determining risk of placement. Others have developed guides to measuring risk of abuse and neglect, a frequent precursor to the decision to place children (McDonnell, 1985; Tatara, 1987). These tools will be examined below.

Family preservation programs have been developed as an alternative for families likely to experience placement of their children. The etiology of the forces leading to potential placement can involve any combination of parental, child, and community problems. Even though predicting placement is difficult and will always involve a certain amount of subjective judgment, a screening procedure needs to be developed that can efficiently distinguish those families with a high risk of child placement from those having a low risk. This intake procedure is the operationalization of the target population definition. The definition of risk needs to be explicit, based upon measurable criteria, and easily applied by referral sources and program staff. It can take the form of a written protocol or checklist.

Meddin (1984) has developed a set of placement criteria based on the questionnaire responses of 81 direct services workers in a major midwestern public child welfare agency. Key factors identified were continued risk of abuse or neglect, severity of the last incident, functioning and cooperation of the caretaker, age of the child, absence of the prime caretaker, previous placements, and a hazardous living environment. These factors were thought to be interactive.

According to Horejsi (1979), risk of imminent placement may be high if any of the following is true:

- A child is in danger of serious physical harm or needs medical attention.
- A child is subject to environmental danger.
- A child is too young or physically unable to escape a dangerous situation.
- A parent or caretaker is exhibiting severe physical or emotional problems.
- A responsible person is unavailable to care for and protect the child.
- A child is asking to be removed.
- A child is exhibiting severe physical or emotional problems.
- Parents are requesting immediate removal of a child.
- Other professionals or agencies are expressing great concern about the safety and welfare of a child.

The Iowa Department of Human Services requires its staff to consider the following factors to determine risk to the child and eligibility for family-centered services (Tatara, 1987, p. 286):

- the nature and seriousness of any immediate presenting problems
- the family's ability to meet basic needs
- the family's involvement with others such as extended family, neighbors, friends, schools, churches, and other organizations
- characteristics of each individual family member that may have contributed to any immediate problems or are impeding a solution
- characteristics of the entire family that may have contributed to any immediate problems or that are impeding a solution
- history of past attempts by the family to solve its problems

Another approach to defining operationally when children are at risk is in terms of their "well-being," as defined on the Child Well-Being Scales (Magura & Moses, 1986). Each of 43 scales "measures a concept that is related to one or more physical, psychological or social needs that all children have: the degree to which this set of needs is met defines a child's state of overall well-being" (p. 83). The scales were developed primarily to serve as a client outcome measure, but all or some could be incorporated into a risk assessment protocol. Each scale has explicitly defined levels ranging from adequate to increasingly higher intervals of inadequate child care.

A new instrument, the Family Risk Scales, has been developed by the Child Welfare League (Magura, Moses, & Jones, 1987). It consists of 28 scales and was designed to measure risk of placement more directly. Five of the scales in this instrument come directly from the Child Well-Being Scales. To date, the Family Risk Scales have not had the extensive testing that the Child Well-Being Scales have had.

## Screening Protocols

Table 2.1 reviews the client screening process for a number of recent family preservation programs with explicit screening criteria cited in the literature.

A risk of placement protocol is necessary for consistent assessment of whether or not a referral should be included in the pool of clients deemed to have at least one child at risk of imminent out-of-home placement. As pointed out earlier, the use of a protocol is important because reliability in worker judgment has been found to be weak or biased by value judgments or personal ideologies. Factors to be considered in such a protocol, such as the one employed by the New Jersey Family Preservation Services program (Feldman, 1987) include, but should not necessarily be limited to, the following:

- certification by the referral source that imminent placement will occur without intervention
- date of referral source's most recent face-to-face contact with the family
- past placement history
- referral source's assessment of potential for physical violence within or toward the family
- referral source's expectations of the family preservation program
- other agency involvement with the family
- result of past interventions with the family
- reason for referral
- information about the current crisis

## Defining "Imminent Risk of Placement"

An imminent event is defined as one that is likely to occur at any moment. Family preservation programs are generally designed to prevent unnecessary placement of children from families that have children at "imminent" risk of placement due to a family crisis. Many family preservation programs are designed to be or are viewed as the preplacement service of last resort. If the intervention is not made at the time of the crisis or the services do not succeed, it is expected that the children identified as at risk would be placed within a very short period of time. The immediacy of placement is a key factor in determining what families are considered part of the at-risk population in most programs designed to prevent placement. In fact, in some jurisdictions, a panel of service providers or the court has to make a formal declaration that placement is the only option for a family's children before they are eligible for intensive in-home services. Operationalizing imminence of placement risk is difficult. Criteria for emergency placement are often included in procedural and policy manuals, but not all cases of removal fall into this category. If a child has not yet been removed, some criteria for imminence of placement risk that are being used include the following:

- *Legal status of the child:* If a petition for dependency has been filed or the child has been declared dependent, degree of risk of removal may be high.
- *Supervisory panel decision:* If a supervisor or placement committee has made the decision to remove, risk of removal may be high.
- *Worker decision:* If a worker has decided to remove, within a specified time frame, unless these services are provided, the risk of removal may be moderate to high, depending upon the local agency's policies and practices.

If imminence is a key screening criterion, then families with long-term problems but without children at risk of harm or not demanding the removal of their children would be considered

**Table 2.1** Screening Criteria and Process of Selected Family Preservation Programs

| Study/Report | Site/Agency Type | Selection Criteria | Exclusions | Selection Process | Referral Sources |
|---|---|---|---|---|---|
| Jones (1985) | New York City 7 public and private agencies | foster care likely within 6 months <br><br> caretakers and problems amenable to preventative services at least one child under 14 years old | active child abuse investigation | two tiered: (1) Department of Social Services (2) prevention agency | Department of Social Services some community agencies |
| Kinney (1978) | Tacoma, WA 1 private agency | family too dysfunctional for traditional services <br><br> agreement among referent, parents, and Homebuilders that this is the last option before placement <br><br> at least one family member expresses a desire to keep family together | high risk of physical danger to staff | direct to Homebuilders 24 hours/day | community agencies self-referral[a] |

| | | | | |
|---|---|---|---|---|
| Landsman (1985) | Wisconsin 14 county/departments social service agencies | all sites define own criteria, e.g., at risk of placement; sexual abuse; preteens at risk; high-risk teens; high-risk pregnant mothers; children up to 9; multi-problem families | direct to program | various: social services medical schools self-referral law enforcement courts relatives |
| Feldman (1987) | New Jersey 4 private agencies under state contract in 4 counties | risk of imminent placement due to: abuse/neglect runaway out-of-control behavior domestic violence delinquency suicidal behavior parental incapacitation all other resources in community failed | program used to stabilize home until placement arranged; extensive placement history; homelessness, if primary problem | two tiered: (1) external screener (2) prevention agency has 3 days to screen case after initial contact | (1) Department of Social Services (2) family crisis intervention (3) regional mental health units; referral source is required to make face-to-face contact with family to discuss willingness to participate |
| AuClaire & Schwartz (1986) | Hennepin County, Minnesota county agency | adolescents 12-17 needing and approved by supervisor for out-of-home placement; not under court-ordered placement state ward | referring agency does internal screening; residential cases also screened by multidisciplinary committee | county Department of Social Services |
| Pecora et al. (1986) | Utah 2 state-run sites | any child or adolescent at risk of placement child safety can be assured | internal screening | Department of Social Services |

a. This program currently accepts referrals only from public agencies that have the responsibility of placing children (D. Haapala, personal communication, 1988).

inappropriate referrals. Children identified and approved for residential placement and awaiting an opening at a facility would also not be eligible. The use of family preservation programs as stopgap service providers, pending out-of-home placement, will skew outcome results.

## Other Populations Appropriate for Family Preservation Services

Some intensive in-home service programs have been expanded or targeted to serve children already in out-of-home placement. These child welfare clients include (a) children designated to return to their parents from foster care and (b) children in foster, preadoptive, or adoptive homes on the verge of placement due to problems comparable to those identified in earlier sections of this chapter. Other non-child welfare populations include families referred by mental health, juvenile justice, education, or drug rehabilitation agencies.

Additional screening criteria need to be developed for such populations. Issues to resolve include identifying the stage of permanence planning when intervention would occur and whether or not the family preservation program would have to be the agency of last resort for foster or adoptive parents.

It is important to detail whom the program is not equipped to serve as well. There are a number of categories of cases that may not be suitable to this short-term intervention model. However, continued empirical study may be necessary to rule out any family problems listed below. In many instances, families with the following problems are either excluded from family preservation programs or have to meet additional criteria. Sometimes these problems are not readily apparent and only become so after intensive intervention has begun. Continuation of the intervention is then decided on a case-by-case basis. Issues that sometimes lead to program exclusion include the following:

- life-threatening abuse of the child by caretakers
- active, serious substance abuse by caretakers
- history of multiple out-of-home placements
- homelessness (if this is the primary factor determining placement)
- serious chronic mental illness or severe retardation of caretakers
- lack of caretaker willing to work with the in-home program

Other characteristics that have been used to screen families out of programs include age of the target child, threat of physical danger to staff, and active child abuse investigation. The use of exclusionary criteria is, as mentioned above, sometimes a part of the program start-up process. Referral program sources and staff may be reluctant to refer or to accept all families during the early stages of a demonstration project, but with increased experience they may either reduce or modify the restrictions.

## *Procedural Considerations*

Once criteria for screening cases have been developed and tested, thought needs to be devoted to the mechanics of making the agencies and workers aware of the program and the process of who, when, and how to refer to the family preservation program.

Education and training can take the form of kickoff meetings with community agencies and the dissemination of videotape presentations. The agency may also wish to use public service announcements, news releases, and the like. An effort should be made to state clearly the prime criteria for referral and any other eligibility criteria that are mandatory. Information packets describing the unique features of the program and eligibility criteria should also be distributed. A common assessment tool will greatly enhance the uniformity of the screeners' decisions and, ideally, every referral source should use the same screening instrument.

Four issues that have an impact on the quality of the referrals are (a) the required standard for the referral source's level of knowledge about, and involvement with, the at-risk family prior to the referral; (b) availability of a trained screener, external to the program, to assess independently the level of placement risk; (c) a second confirmatory screening completed by the family preservation program staff; and (d) limitation of referrals to a few designated community agencies.

A screening process that requires a referral source to have recent, face-to-face contact with the target family has two benefits. It will ensure that current information is available about the family and that the family members will have learned about the program and expressed their feelings about participation.

A trained screener or placement committee, external to the program, can add objectivity and reliability to the referral process. The screener would be responsible for determining whether or not a new referral meets all agency criteria and whether or not there is evidence of high placement risk if intensive intervention is not begun. An external screening body can also diffuse predictable community hostility when referred cases are rejected for not meeting the established criteria.

If an external screening process is used, it is essential that a second-stage screening occur at the program. In some programs, clients are terminated within three days of referral if it is felt that a child is at extreme risk of harm while remaining at home or if the family cannot be engaged in the treatment process. Other programs conduct postreferral evaluations for much longer periods of time if the family is difficult to engage. Feedback to the referral source and screener is essential to increase case uniformity. It is also important for the evaluator to gather information about these second-stage dropouts to determine if they have characteristics that set them apart from the families receiving services.

A more orderly referral process with greater consistency of referrals will ensue if the number of referral sources is limited. The designation of limited referral sources, especially to those with the authority to place children, can aid the reinforcement of appropriate referrals and help reduce the need to debate client eligibility.

In-home programs that are the service of last resort will especially benefit from this funneling of referrals. Contingencies should be worked out, however, when a referral source such as the family court mandates acceptance of a family into the program regardless of referral criteria.

Once a protocol is developed, pilot testing and calibration of the instrument are vital. If external screeners are used, their training can be used to calibrate the protocol using vignettes based on actual case histories of families with children at risk of placement. Periodic reviews with screeners and program staff during the course of the evaluation are also recommended.

## *Conclusion*

Careful definition of the target population is a factor that is essential to successful evaluation. The definition of the target population affects an evaluator's ability to carry out the following tasks:

- determining whether or not the program is reaching the families to which it is addressed
- developing a client typology—identifying the types of clients most likely to benefit from the program
- conducting comparisons with other client samples of the program over time
- conducting comparisons with other programs using similar or traditional service approaches

Early involvement of the evaluator in the program development cycle can aid in the construction of tightly drawn definitions and case selection criteria of target clients. Characteristics of target clients must be explicitly described in measurable terms. The adherence to these criteria by referents and program staff should be measured by the evaluator during the course of the evaluation.

The determination of risk of out-of-home placement is based on an assessment of multiple parent, child, and family factors within an ecological context. These factors include the following:

- characteristics of children, caretakers, and family—age range, placement history, disabilities
- the potential harm to the children—type of precipitating problems, severity of the problems
- the willingness of the family to provide care and/or protection—court involvement, cooperation with the helping agency
- the ability of the family to provide care and/or protection—problem chronicity, homelessness, financial problems, substance abuse
- the level of community and social supports—high-risk environments, level of stress, agency capabilities, utilization of social supports, exhaustion of other community resources

The assessment of placement imminence is integral to the screening process in many programs. Waiting lists are antithetical to crisis intervention programs.

Characteristics making families ineligible for in-home services have to be defined and made part of the screening criteria. Active substance abuse by a caretaker, history of multiple-out-of-home placements, chronicity of problems, or serious incapacity of a caretaker may cause a family to be excluded.

Issues that have an impact on the quality of the referrals made to the program include the following:

- the referral source's level of knowledge and involvement with the family prior to referral
- the engagement of trained screeners external to the program
- the use of common assessment tools or protocols
- the use of a confirmatory screening by the family preservation program in tandem with external screeners
- restriction of referrals to a few designated community agencies

# *References*

AuClaire, P., & Schwartz, I. (1986). *An evaluation of the effectiveness of intensive home-based services as an alternative to placement for adolescents and their families.* Minneapolis: Hennepin County Community Services Department and University of Minnesota, Hubert H. Humphrey Institute of Public Affairs.

Barth, R., & Berry, M. (1987). Outcome of child welfare services under permanency planning. *Social Service Review, 61,* 71-90.

Belsky, J. (1978). Three theoretical models of child abuse: A critical review. *Child Abuse and Neglect, 2,* 37-49.

Bronfenbrenner, U. (1979). *The ecology of human development: Experiences by nature and design.* Cambridge, MA: Harvard University Press.

Camasso, M. J., & Wilkinson, K. P. (in press). Severe child maltreatment in ecological perspective: The case of the western energy boom. *Social Service Review.*

Feldman, L. H. (1987, September). *Evaluating family-based programs within an ecological context.* Paper presented at the conference, "Empowering Families: A Celebration of Family Based Services," Minneapolis.

Garbarino, J., & Sherman, D. (1980). High risk neighborhoods and high risk families: The human ecology of child maltreatment. *Child Development, 51,* 188-198.

Gruber, M. L. (1980). Inequality in the social services. *Social Service Review, 54,* 59-75.

Hargreaves, W. A., & Attkisson, C. C. (1978). Evaluating program outcomes. In C. C. Attkisson, W. A. Hargreaves, M. J. Horowitz, & J. E. Sorensen (Eds.), *Evaluation of human service programs* (pp. 303-340). New York: Academic Press.

Hinckley, E. C. (1984). Homebuilders: The Maine experience. *Children Today, 13*(5), 14-17.

Horejsi, C. (1979). *Foster family care: A handbook for social workers, allied professionals and concerned citizens.* Springfield, IL: Charles C. Thomas.

Horowitz, B., & Wolock, I. (1981). Maternal deprivation, child maltreatment, and agency intervention among poor families. In L. H. Pelton (Ed.), *The social context of child abuse and neglect* (pp. 137-184). New York: Human Sciences Press.

Jones, M. A. (1985). *A second chance for families.* New York: Child Welfare League of America.

Kinney, J. (1978). Homebuilders: An in-home crisis intervention program. *Children Today, 7,* 15-17, 35.

Leeds, S. (1986). *Promoting family stability: Final report of the New Jersey performance contracting study.* Trenton: Bureau of Research, Evaluation and Quality Assurance, New Jersey Division of Youth and Family Services.

Lloyd, J. C., & Bryce, M. E. (1984). *Placement prevention and family reunification: A handbook for the family centered service practitioner.* Iowa City: University of Iowa, National Resource Center on Family Based Services.

Magura, S. (1981). Are services to prevent foster care effective? *Children and Youth Services Review, 3,* 193-212.

Magura, S., & Moses, B. S. (1986). *Outcome measures for child welfare services: Theory and applications.* Washington, DC: Child Welfare League of America.

Magura, S., Moses, B. S., & Jones, M. A. (1987). *Assessing risk and measuring changes in the family.* Washington, DC: Child Welfare League of America.

McDonnell, P. (1985). *Children at risk: Decision criteria for removal and/or return home.* Chicago and Chapel Hill: Taylor Institute of Chicago and University of North Carolina, School of Social Work.

Meddin, B. J. (1984). Criteria for placement decisions in protective services. *Child Welfare, 63,* 367-373.

Polansky, N., Ammons, P. W., & Gaudin, J. M. (1985) Loneliness and isolation in child neglect. *Social Casework, 66,* 38-47.

Polansky, N., Gaudin, J. M., Ammons, P. W., & Davis, K. B. (1985) The psychological ecology of the neglectful mother. *Child Abuse and Neglect, 9,* 265-275.

Riecken, H. W., & Boruch, R. F. (Eds.). (1974). *Social experimentation: A method for planning and evaluating social intervention.* New York: Academic Press.

Rossi, P. H., Freeman, H. E., & Wright, S. R. (1979). *Evaluation: A systematic approach.* Beverly Hills, CA: Sage.

Segal, U. A., & Schwartz, S. (1985). Factors affecting placement decisions of children following short-term emergency care. *Child Abuse and Neglect, 9,* 543-548.

Siegel, L. M., Attkisson, C. C., & Carson, L. G. (1978). Assessment of community service needs. In C. C. Attkisson, W. A. Hargreaves, M. J. Horowitz, & J. E. Sorensen (Eds.), *Evaluation of human service programs* (pp. 215-252). New York: Academic Press.

Spearly, J. L., & Lauderdale, J. L. (1983). Community characteristics and ethnicity in the prediction of child maltreatment rates. *Child Abuse and Neglect, 7,* 91-105.

Stein, T. J. (1985). Projects to prevent out-of-home placements. *Children and Youth Services Review, 7,* 109-121.

Stein, T. J., & Rzepnicki, T. E. (1983). *Decision making at child welfare intake: A handbook for practitioners.* New York: Child Welfare League of America.

Tatara, T. (1987). An overview of current practices in CPS risk assessment and family systems assessment in public child welfare. In T. Tatara (Ed.), *A summary of the highlights of the national roundtable on CPS risk assessment and family systems assessment* (pp. 415-462). Washington, DC: American Public Welfare Association.

Yuan, Y. Y., & McDonald, W. R. (1987). *AB 1562 demonstration projects: Year one report.* Sacramento, CA: Walter R. McDonald & Associates, Inc.

## 3

# *Program Environment and Organization*

### KRISTINE E. NELSON

Programs providing services to families and children differ along many dimensions. Evaluators must accurately describe the components of the particular program being studied, both to increase understanding of the service and to enable comparison among programs. Description of the program should include its history, context, and current operations, and may involve both qualitative and quantitative measures. The history and context of the program cover its goals and objectives, auspices and stage of development, organizational structure and financing, and community context. The description of current operations should consider the program's philosophy and model of service, its structure and staffing, the pattern of service delivery, and methods of reporting and accountability. Employing measures that have already proven useful in other studies of family and children's services will conserve scarce resources for evaluation and increase comparability across programs.

Programs providing family and children's services differ along many dimensions. Precise description of the program's organization and environment is necessary to assure that both internal and external audiences understand the nature of the program being evaluated. Program description takes on extra importance among relatively new programs that are still taking shape, such as family preservation services. The program description may be qualitative or quantitative in nature, depending on the design and purpose of the evaluation. Many aspects of the program will not vary by case, by worker, or by office, and describing them will not be complicated unless several different programs are being compared.

This chapter will assume that the evaluation being conducted is of a single program and will treat most aspects of the program qualitatively rather than quantitatively. The first section of the chapter deals with the program's history and context; the second section addresses documenting program operations.

## *Program History and Context*

In any evaluation project, but particularly with new services, it is important to understand the history and context of the program being evaluated. This includes program goals and objectives, the auspices and stage of development of the program, the community context in which the program operates, and the organizational structure and financing of the program. This information can be obtained most easily by interviewing key informants and analyzing existing written materials such as grant applications, annual reports, program histories, or previous evaluations.

Optimally, informants will include the people involved in the establishment of the program, the top administrator with direct responsibility for the program, the person in charge of supervising the program on a daily basis, the program staff, representatives from other agencies in the community, and a sample of families, if this is possible. A formal interview schedule is not required, but it is helpful to have a detailed list of questions and to keep careful notes of, or to dictate, the contents of each interview soon after it is concluded (Patton, 1980).

### Program Goals and Objectives

Goals and objectives may emanate from several different sources: the framers of the program, the legislation or legal mandate, those who planned and implemented the program, and/or the key actors currently involved in the program. Family and children's programs have been initiated at community, state, and federal levels. The birth of such a program often depends on the efforts of a small group of activists with a particular goal, often to improve service to clients. To realize this goal, they involve key people in the community whose support is necessary to initiate a new program. Conflicting goals often appear at this stage (Etzioni, 1969; Wildavsky, 1972). For example, a program administrator may want to establish an alternative to emergency shelter care and eventual placement of status offenders in her community. To gain administrative and legislative support for a family preservation program, she may "sell" it on the basis that it costs less than placement. Thus two potentially conflicting goals are present at the outset: improved service to families and reduction of program costs.

Often goals are global and reflect the formal language of enabling legislation. Stating goals at a high level of abstraction is important in gaining support for programs, but it is troublesome for evaluators, especially if the goals are conflicting or the claims made for the program are inflated (Morell, 1982; Rossi & Wright, 1977, p. 10). However, operational goals established in the process of planning and implementing the program, if stated in measurable terms, may be of great assistance in evaluating the program (Sorensen & Elpers, 1978; Van Maanen, 1979).

Sometimes very specific goals are mandated in the legislation, administrative rules, or purchase of service contract that governs the program. For example, California, Michigan, Connecticut, and several other states have specified that the goal of their family preservation initiatives is the prevention of placement of abused and neglected children.

In determining the main audience for the evaluation, it is important for the evaluator to identify the degree of consensus on goals among the program's initiators and current participants, "hidden" agendas or goals that may be affecting the program, and any conflict between the formal program goals and the goals of individuals. If the program supervisor is concerned about the effectiveness of particular intervention treatment technologies with families and the program administrator is concerned about documenting cost savings, the evaluator has to determine which concern is primary in order to design an effective and efficient research methodology.

Finally, the evaluator needs to assess the impact on the program of various goal statements and definitions. Have they been implemented or ignored? Is there a logical relationship between the program's goals and its structure and operation? Are objectives clearly defined and their achievement monitored? Do the participants merely assume goals are being met because staff are working and funds are being expended, or do they receive information documenting goal achievement? In short, how accountable is the program already and in what areas?

### Auspices and Stage of Development of the Program

Establishing the program's history and goals includes identifying the auspices and stage of development of the program. The various stages in program development have been characterized as planning, implementation, and stabilization or maturity (e.g., Neugeborn, 1985, p. 84; Tripodi, Fellin, & Epstein, 1978). Depending on the stage of development, an evaluation of the program may be formative or summative, process or outcome oriented (Herman, Morris, & Fitz-Gibbon, 1987; Tripodi et al., 1978). In the planning stages, evaluators have the advantage of attempting to establish clear and measurable definitions of program components, to build reliable and valid measurement tools into the monitoring and reporting procedures, and to define the target population and objectives of the program unambiguously. Most evaluations start at a later stage, however, and must attempt to impose clarity on concepts and procedures already in use.

At any stage of program development, it is important to ascertain whether a process- or outcome-oriented evaluation is desired (see Jacobs, 1988, for an analysis of different levels of evaluation). If the main question concerns assessment of program implementation, then process issues such as number and source of referrals, the population being served, intake and assessment procedures, patterns of contacts, and participants' satisfaction and dissatisfaction are paramount (Roberts-Gray & Scheirer, 1988). Formative or process evaluation may help to modify the program or its implementation by focusing on the delivery of specific services to a target population, issues that are covered in other chapters of this volume. Questions of effectiveness and goal achievement require measurement and evaluation of family and program outcomes, which are also addressed in later chapters.

There are several specific issues that must be taken into account, depending on whether the program is located in a public or private agency. For example, in public agencies a primary audience of an evaluation may be the legislative or executive body that funds the program, whether or not they have requested or are involved in the evaluation (see Hedrick, 1988). For private agencies, a primary audience may be the local department of social services that purchases their services. More clearly defined policies and procedures in public agencies may make it easier to describe and evaluate the program, or they may create obstacles to obtaining informed consent from participants or randomly assigning them to different treatment groups. In addition, although familiarity with written policies and procedures is desirable, it may prove a formidable task in a large public bureaucracy.

Again, depending on the agency's auspices, relationships with other programs and units in the agency may vary. Specialized programs in public agencies may be misunderstood and underutilized because they operate under different assumptions and conditions than most public social services. Direct recruitment and staffing of cases from other units or programs, case coordination, consultation on unreferred cases, and participation on review committees may help link and interpret the specialized program to others within and outside the agency. These linkages can be described and assessed. While a program under private auspices also may be located in a multiservice agency, its funds and referrals might come directly from a public agency. Therefore, working relationships with the public agency may be more intense than with the other units in the agency.

## Organizational Structure

Whether the program is a component of a traditional child welfare, social service, or mental health agency, or whether the entire agency operates from an ecological, family-oriented perspective is critical (Hutchinson & Nelson, 1985). Competing treatment philosophies, program standards, service goals, and personnel policies make the evaluator's task more difficult and the position of the program and its formal and informal relationships within the "host" agency crucial.

For example, in public social service agencies, intensive family services may be a primary subdivision reporting directly to a division head, a unit within a placement alternatives subdivision that includes paraprofessional services and less restrictive placement alternatives, or a unit within a more traditional child and family subdivision that includes child protective services, ongoing family services, and placement units. Private agencies typically have a less hierarchical organization, with more equal and independent units reporting directly to the executive officer. In either situation, unless there is an integrated intake unit that has a clear understanding of family preservation services and strong assessment skills, families may experience a number of transfers and long delays before reaching the specialized unit. Some agencies have addressed this problem by adopting a family-based perspective throughout the organization, so that all services support the ultimate goal of family preservation.

Regardless of the type of organization, the position and influence of the program's primary administrator and his or her commitment to the service may do much to determine the flow of funds and information to and from the program. The degree of understanding and support of other administrators and units can help or hinder the program in myriad ways. The availability of other in-house services and cooperation and coordination with their providers may also influence client outcomes. Placement review committees or quality-control procedures can provide valuable consultation or make life miserable for workers. Drawing an ecomap of the program's relationships with other units and important agencies in the external environment may help to clarify which, if any, need to be scrutinized in the evaluation process (Lauffer, 1984).

## Community Context

Interactions with the community are important in a number of ways. Indeed, depending on the purpose and nature of the evaluation, outside agencies and bodies may need to be surveyed or key informants interviewed as part of the evaluation. There may have been a high level of community participation and consultation in the development of the program that facilitated acceptance of the program in the community and stimulated a flow of referrals. The community's knowledge and support of the program and cooperation in case planning for families depends on the development and maintenance of these linkages. Relationships with the courts, the police, health or mental health agencies, other social service agencies, or citizen groups may be crucial in securing an adequate number of referrals or in avoiding pressure to accept more cases than the program can effectively serve (see, e.g., Cowen, 1978, p. 803).

In addition, the availability of supportive and concrete services in a community may profoundly affect the structure and functioning of the program. In an environment rich with counseling, supportive, and concrete services, a family and children's program may specialize in a particular problem or target population. In an isolated rural area, more comprehensive services may need to be provided. Thus availability and accessibility of complementary services are of central importance in evaluating implementation and outcomes

(Feldman, 1987, p. 14; Hinckley & Ellis, 1985; Jones, Magura, & Shyne, 1981).

The presence of competing or similar services in the community may also affect the form and function of a particular program. Private agencies may vie for referrals and scarce purchase-of-service dollars. Public agency programs may fear the competition of private programs, with their greater flexibility in service delivery and personnel policies, or agencies may develop a formal or informal division of labor, with, for example, one agency offering in-office services and specializing in families with adolescent offenders or problems such as sexual abuse and another focusing on in-home services to families with problems of abuse or neglect of younger children. Whatever the main focus, most programs need to maintain a broad expertise in order to be able to assess and address the needs of all family members either directly or through referral.

Finally, many programs regard the community as a target of change as well as a resource. Individuals and organizations in the community may need to change their attitudes or behaviors toward a family in order to facilitate family change. Effective workers do not shy away from this charge or help families adjust to their circumstances, no matter how egregious. New services or changes in existing services may be required to meet program goals. Again, this should be recognized and evaluated as an important part of the service (e.g., Feldman, 1987). Both overall program goals and objectives and specific case objectives should be assessed for content on community change.

## Financial Support

The sources and stability of funds affect whether or not a program is implemented as planned and is able to meet its goals and objectives. The following questions help to identify financial issues needing further investigation:

- Is the program funded by grants, as a demonstration project, or as a pilot program, or is it part of the agency's established services or approach?
- Is funding long term or year to year?
- Have there been changes in the political or economic environment that threaten the availability of funds?
- Do funders need assurance on particular aspects of the program to continue to fund?
- Are their expectations of the program realistic?
- Are funds adequate for the size of the program in terms of staff, clients currently served, and the extent of need in the target population?
- Are funds sufficient to attract and retain competent and qualified staff?
- Does the program need additional money to expand the type or scope of services offered?
- Does the program have more money or staff than it can effectively use?
- Does the relative allocation of resources to different services and activities within the program, agency, and community make sense in terms of family and community needs?
- Are standards and procedures for financial accountability adequate?
- Who participates in budgetary decision making and who should?

Seldom are these questions easy to answer unequivocally, but they are literally the "bottom line" in most evaluation efforts, whether overtly or covertly. Chapter 6 of this volume deals with some of these issues in more depth.

### *Program Operations*

Day-to-day program operations are the main substance of an evaluation, whether its purpose is to describe and document the actual implementation of the program or to analyze outcomes. The main areas considered in this chapter are philosophy and model of service, structure and staffing, the pattern of service delivery, and reporting and accountability. Some aspects of program operation may be the same from office to office, from staff to staff, and from family to family, while others may vary. Depending on the stability of the program component and the purpose of the evaluation, qualitative or quantitative measures may be preferred. Interviews, direct observation, and evaluation of written materials are all qualitative methods of data collection that can be employed in studying program operations (Manning, 1982; Marshall & Rossman, 1989; Patton, 1980). However, some aspects of the program will require a more structured approach, including, for example, surveys of staff or cooperating agencies in the community or structured interviews with families.

Any information that is to be used in a statistical analysis must be quantified and, therefore, recorded or subsequently coded using some common unit of measurement such as hours, years, or number of occurrences, or using a scale with exhaustive and mutually exclusive categories. The development of quantitative measures can be quite time-consuming, so scales that have already been employed in family and children's service evaluations should be used when available. Moos (1988) cites a number of scales useful in studying program environments. The Family Based Services Inventory, developed by the National Resource Center on Family Based Services, also contains measures of a broad range of program issues (Nelson, Emlen, Hutchinson, & Landsman, 1988). Cross-study comparisons using similar measures allow knowledge concerning services to cumulate, rather than be locked into idiosyncratic measures in individual studies.

**Philosophy and Model of Service**

Although a philosophy and model of service are usually implied from the start of a program, they can change over time through attrition or the influence of other approaches. Thus it is important to identify assumptions about families and change, the intervention theory and approach, key values directing the program, outside sources of consultation and inspiration, and the degree of consensus on these issues, both initially and over time. Open-ended interviews will be most useful in establishing the original philosophy and models and changes over time, but quantitative measures may be necessary if there are differences among staff or too many staff to interview, or if correlation to outcome or comparison to other programs is desired.

For example, there are several models of intensive family services and several theoretical approaches to intervention. Among the models most often replicated are the Homebuilders learning theory-based model and the family-systems model first employed in Iowa and Oregon (Nelson, Landsman, & Deutelbaum, 1990). While key values of working with the family as a whole, recognizing and building on family strengths, and empowering and preserving families are common across programs, assumptions about effective interventions to promote family change vary. A useful codification of attributes of family-based services was developed by the Social Research Institute at the University of Utah and has been used in cross-agency studies (AuClaire & Schwartz, 1986; Nelson et al., 1988; Pecora, Fraser, Haapala, & Bartlome, 1987). It lists 14 possible attributes of intensive family services and asks respondents to rate their importance using a Likert scale. This scale identifies attributes believed to be most important in a particular program and enables comparison with other programs. The items are as follows:

- The program provides delivery of "hard" services, such as moving, cleaning, grocery shopping with clients.
- The program asks clients to identify/determine and prioritize their own treatment goals.
- Workers are available 24 hours a day for emergency visits or calls.
- The program refers families to other counseling services.
- Services are routinely provided in the home.
- Services are routinely provided at night or on weekends.

- Client appointments are at the convenience of the families.
- Initial contact with clients is made within 24 hours of the referral.
- Services are brief in duration, lasting no more than 90 days.
- Services are intense, provided two or three times a week for 1-4 hours per time.
- "Nonmotivated" clients are accepted for service.
- The philosophy of service providers is that most children are better off in their own homes.
- Service providers encourage families to assume greater responsibility and self-determination over their own lives (family empowerment).
- Services are focused on goal-oriented case plans.

Programs and practitioners also vary in the intervention theories and practices that they employ. For example, the entire program may subscribe to a behavioral or family systems approach and/or individual workers may prefer different theoretical orientations. The National Resource Center on Family Based Services has employed a series of scales developed by Hamilton and Montayne that identify preferences for a psychodynamic, behavioral, communications, strategic, or structural approach to family intervention (Nelson et al., 1988). Although workers tested to date seem to be eclectic in their treatment philosophies, these scales may be useful in describing the various treatment approaches employed in programs.

**Structural Issues**

Program structure shapes service delivery and has a strong influence on outcomes, regardless of treatment philosophy. Some of the issues relating to public and private auspices have already been discussed. The location of service, caseload size, intensity and pattern of contacts, average length of service, and accessibility and physical accommodations of the program are also of central importance. Although many of these will be taken up in further detail in other chapters, a brief discussion is warranted here.

Although structure is determined by agency policy, families' experiences in the program may vary and thus need to be measured. For example, while some intensive family service programs deliver services primarily in the home and use office contacts for specific purposes, others deliver services primarily in the office and make home visits for assessment. The number and frequency of in-home and in-office contacts may differ among families, and, depending on the treatment issues addressed, the location of visits may be related to outcome. It is important, also, to distinguish between in-office service delivery and the use of the office for special tasks such as meeting with other service providers or completing legal documents related to placement.

Caseloads will vary depending on whether each child at risk of placement is considered a case or whether the family as a whole is counted as a case. Location of service delivery may also affect caseloads, with in-office programs serving more families and in-home programs, especially those that require workers to travel great distances, having smaller caseloads. In addition, the intensity and duration of service affects caseload size; programs with more frequent contact over a short period generally have smaller caseloads, often only two or three families per worker. If cases are seen for assessment only or if reunification services involve the family, the placement setting, and other services, caseloads may be affected. Caseload size, intensity, and duration, therefore, are interrelated and should be documented. In addition, intensity and length of service may vary among families and may be related to outcome, and so should be recorded for each family. Ways of recording this information are discussed in Chapter 4 of this volume.

The pattern of contacts may also vary over the period of service, thus averages may be misleading. For example, in a three-month intensive family service program, contacts may be most frequent in the first month of service and taper off thereafter. Different patterns can reflect either a planful approach to intensity or, as one study found, a system that is still oriented to delivering the most intensive services only when placement is a reality rather than a possibility (Leeds, 1987). Length and pattern of contacts may also be related to the program's policies and procedures, such as a formal time limit or a periodic review process that encourages termination within a specific time frame. It is particularly important to assess the impact of such constraints on service effectiveness (Jones et al., 1981; Nelson et al., 1988).

Finally, the accessibility of services with regard to location, hours, and emergency provisions; the physical accommodations, such as space, decor, and accessibility to handicapped clients; and special facilities such as one-way mirrors, videotaping capacity, child care, and transportation should be documented. It is important both to describe the agency policies and facilities and to assess their utilization. For example, an agency may provide for 24-hour access, but clients may seldom be seen late at night or on weekends. If special equipment such as one-way mirrors and videotape cameras are available, the evaluation might assess whether or not they are being used appropriately. Staff's assessment of their need for and satisfaction with office space might be solicited, as well as clients' evaluation of the accessibility, convenience, and comfort of services and facilities (e.g., see Laughlin & Weiss, 1981). Finally, if an office-based program does not provide handicapped access, child care, and transportation, the impact on actual and potential clients should be assessed through surveys or analysis of existing utilization and population data.

### Staffing

In many respects, staffing is at the heart of family and children's services in terms of both quality and cost. Evaluators should describe for both line and administrative staff minimum and average qualifications in terms of education and experience; procedures for orienting new staff; continuing in-service training, staffing, and supervision patterns; and rates and reasons for turnover (Peterson & Bickman, 1988). While, again, much of this may be described qualitatively, it is important to document the frequency with which desired characteristics occur and to assess staff perception of and satisfaction with personnel issues.

Policies and procedures regarding hiring and staff characteristics such as ethnicity, age, education, and experience may be derived from existing records or determined through a survey. While staff characteristics have shown little relationship to case outcome (e.g., see Pecora et al., 1987), they affect the consistency of the program, its ability to deliver particular kinds of services, and the perception of the program in the community. Staffing issues may vary between public and private agencies. Public agencies have to deal with more rigid personnel policies, while private agencies may not be able to pay salaries that attract highly qualified staff. At the very least, years and type of education (including professional education) and years of experience in family-oriented, child welfare, and public social services should be measured.

*Training.* Even qualified staff require in-service training. Most programs provide an orientation to agency policies and procedures, but when a particular treatment approach and philosophy are involved, more extensive training is needed (Hinckley & Ellis, 1985). When programs are established, outside consultants are commonly brought in to train staff. Often, however, only the original staff are trained, and new staff may be insufficiently prepared for their responsibilities. This may be exacerbated by a lack of both workers and supervisors who are educated and/or experienced in the type of services the program provides. Thus the type and quantity of preservice and in-service training should be documented, as well as workers' assessments of the adequacy of their preparation and continued opportunities for education. Ideally, training in theoretical approach, practical application and skills, and program policies and procedures should be assessed separately (Pecora, Delewski, Booth, Haapala, & Kinney, 1985).

*Staffing patterns.* Staffing patterns should be related to required qualifications, in-service training, and sizes of caseloads. Various types of direct service staff may be employed in family and children's services, including the following:

- *paraprofessional staff:* usually local residents or volunteers with limited prior formal training who provide support, skills training (e.g., household skills, parent education, money management), or role modeling to families
- *entry-level professional staff:* college graduates who may or may not have formal professional training (e.g., BSW degree) and who provide casework, case management, or supportive services
- *trained professional staff:* workers with graduate degrees (e.g., MSW or counseling degree) who do assessment, case planning, and individual, family, and/or couple counseling
- *specialized professional staff:* professionally educated workers (e.g., family therapists) with additional training in specific interventions and theories (e.g., behavioral, structural, or strategic family therapy)

For descriptive purposes, the number and types of professional, paraprofessional, and support staff and volunteers should be documented, as well as the ratio of supervisors and clerical workers to direct service staff, professional to paraprofessional staff, and direct service staff to families. Also helpful is a description of how cases are allocated (e.g., on the basis of catchment areas, worker preference or expertise, or availability) and how responsibilities are allocated among different types of staff. If a mixture of staffing patterns is employed, it may be possible to determine what kinds of staffing patterns are used with what kinds of families, and their relative effectiveness.

Although the pattern of assigning a single worker to each family and providing individual supervision is followed in some programs, others employ teaming. With the exception of recent evidence that teaming is more effective with certain family problems (Showell, Hartley, & Allen, 1988), the effectiveness of various staffing patterns is largely unknown. Therefore, the amount and nature of teaming and its relationship to outcome should be documented. Teams may consist of professionally trained workers or a combination of professional and paraprofessional workers. Cotherapy with two professionals is the most expensive form of teaming, although costs may be offset by providing in-office services with higher caseloads. Team consultation on cases seen primarily by a single worker is also a common staffing pattern in intensive family services.

Finally, although the primary roles and functions of different staff positions may be identified in job descriptions, the positions may include additional responsibilities. For example, in crisis-oriented family preservation programs or those located in rural settings, trained professional and family therapy staff may take on the responsibilities of case management, family support, and education. Teaming that includes different levels of staff may also blur roles and functions as specified on paper.

*Supervision.* Supervision may be individual, group, team, peer, or a combination of these methods. Program supervision may be separate from clinical supervision, which in some programs is provided by an external consultant. Clinical supervision may also be provided by supervisory staff who have received specialized training in clinical supervision or by experienced clinicians hired as supervisors. In some programs, no formal provision is made for clinical supervision. Given the complexity of treatment issues and the demanding nature of the problems presented to family and children's services, clinical supervision may be an important factor in providing successful services.

*Morale and turnover.* Turnover has been a vexing problem in children's and family services. Since training and replacement costs are high, in addition to indirect costs to families and service teams, it is important to document the level of, reasons for, and measures taken to minimize turnover. Issues related to turnover include the general level of morale and job satisfaction, pressures in providing particular kinds of services, and opportunities for advancement (Hinckley, 1984; Hinckley & Ellis, 1985; Jayaratne & Chess, 1984). Established measures of job satisfaction and burnout in the social services include Maslach and Jackson's (1981) Human Services Survey and Jayaratne and Chess's (1984) Professional Satisfaction Inventory.

A positive reason for turnover is the range of employment opportunities in mental health services and private practice for workers highly skilled in family interventions. These opportunities may be enticing because family and children's services are more stressful or because of low salaries and lack of nonadministrative career ladders. There may be no career ladder at all for paraprofessionals. The impact of these factors on employment decisions should be explored, especially if turnover is a problem.

## Service Delivery

Specific measures of service delivery are described in Chapter 4, but as part of the overall analysis of the program, the flow of clients through the program should be documented. To identify problems in client flow, it is often helpful to illustrate graphically the sources of referrals, entrance points into the program, concurrent services received by families, and exit points and destinations (Hutchinson, 1983). For example, there may be too few referrals or too many inappropriate referrals, which may require exploration with referral agencies of their perceptions of and satisfaction with the program. Or there may be a long delay between referral to the agency and referral to the worker.

Other programmatic issues in service delivery include timing of services, assessment and case planning, coordination of services, and completion rates. Identifying the average and extreme lag times between the steps of problem identification, referral, first contact, last contact, closing, and follow-up can pinpoint problems in service delivery. Many workers report that families new to services are easier to work with, and research confirms that both prior service and placement histories are associated with placement in intensive family service programs (Landsman, 1985; Leeds, 1984; Nelson et al., 1988; Rzepnicki, 1987). Timing of services thus may be an important determinant of outcome and should be documented.

Assessment, case planning, individualized case objectives, and coordination of services are also important in family preservation services (AuClaire & Schwartz, 1986; Heying, 1985; Nelson et al., 1988; Pecora et al., 1985; Rzepnicki, 1987). Programs using an ecological and family empowerment perspective may involve many people in these activities. Identifying the roles, responsibilities, and influence of workers, other providers, family members, and outside actors such as the court or police will reveal whether these processes are operating according to the philosophy and service model of the program. Questions meriting attention include formal requirements for case plans and the specificity of case objectives, the participation of family members in setting case objectives, the influence of referring workers, the location of case management responsibility, the type and adequacy of case coordination with other providers, and participation and relative influence of various parties in decisions to terminate services or place a child. Several of these factors have been found to influence case outcomes in intensive family services (AuClaire & Schwartz, 1986; Leeds, 1987; Nelson et al., 1988).

Finally, it is important to document completion rates and reasons for client attrition at each point in the service delivery process. Client motivation is an important factor in the success of social services, and many clients are difficult to engage in treatment. Evaluators should attempt to identify specific barriers to client participation and stumbling blocks along the way. Both premature termination and lengthy extension of services to families should be examined (AuClaire & Schwartz, 1986; DeWitt, 1980; Nelson et al., 1988). Since it may be unrealistic to expect some families to be completely independent of all social services after intervention, continuing services should be documented and their appropriateness assessed.

## Reporting and Accountability

The final area addressed is the mechanism for continuing communication and feedback about process and outcomes. All agencies have monitoring and reporting requirements, but many provide little information other than how many families are being served and how much money is being spent. To facilitate efficient management, good supervision, and ongoing evaluation, much more information, in a retrievable form, is usually needed. Thus a description of provisions for administrative or program reporting, case recording, external and internal review, and formal evaluation may be helpful. Again, this information may be gathered through interviews and review of program documents or staff surveys to assess how the procedures are facilitating or hindering work at the direct service level.

The evaluation should document the type and frequency of reporting required by each body to which the agency is accountable, the nature and quality of feedback about the reports, and the type and utility of the agency's management information system. Many direct service workers in public agencies find themselves feeding large quantities of information into a system with no usable return. Program supervisors have begun experimenting with personal computers to increase the amount and flexibility of service information for day-to-day management and supervision (Hedlund, Vieweg, & Cho, 1985; Taylor, 1981).

Case recording is often an issue, especially when workers have large caseloads. In some family and children's services, however, case recording serves a clinical as well as an administrative function and, structured properly, can provide information for ongoing evaluation of the program (Alter & Evens, in press). The evaluation should document the frequency and forms required in case recording and assess both quality-control mechanisms and compliance with the requirements. An audit of the flow of paperwork may reveal redundancies and outdated requirements, opening the way for more efficient collection of needed data. Similarly, an examination of supervisory reviews, administrative reviews, and review boards may point to areas in which efficiency can be improved. This may help to reduce competition between families and paperwork for workers' time and to increase information for monitoring or accountability under purchase-of-service contracts.

## Conclusion

This review has highlighted issues of importance in evaluating the history, context, and program operations of family and children's services. In designing an effective study the evaluator must pay particular attention to the following questions:

- What is the primary audience for the evaluation?
- Should the evaluation be formative (process oriented) or summative (outcome oriented)?
- Which of the program goals should be the primary focus of the evaluation?
- How much detail is needed to describe the program and what are the best ways of gathering this information (e.g., documents, interviews, observations)?
- Are there existing measurement tools that can be used to save time and to allow cross-program comparison of findings?
- What perspectives are needed for a complete picture of the program: those of administrators, supervisors, family-based and support staff, staff in other units, families, other agencies and individuals in the community?

## References

Alter, C. F., & Evens, W. (in press). *Evaluate your practice: A guide to self-assessment.* New York: Springer.

AuClaire, P., & Schwartz, I. (1986). *An evaluation of the effectiveness of intensive home-based services as an alternative to placement for adolescents and their families.* Minneapolis: Hennepin County Community Services Department and University of Minnesota, Hubert H. Humphrey Institute of Public Affairs.

Cowen, E. L. (1978). Some problems in community program evaluation research. *Journal of Consulting and Clinical Psychology, 46,* 792-805.

DeWitt, K. N. (1980). The effectiveness of family therapy: A review of outcome research. *Family Psychotherapy, 2,* 437-465.

Etzioni, A. (1969). Two approaches to organizational analysis: A critique and a suggestion. In H. C. Schulberg, A. Sheldon, & F. Baker (Eds.), *Program evaluation in the health fields* (pp. 101-120). New York: Behavioral Publications.

Feldman, L. (1987, September). *Evaluating family-based service programs within an ecological context*. Paper presented at the conference, "Empowering Families: A Celebration of Family Based Services," Minneapolis.

Hedlund, J. L., Vieweg, B. W., & Cho, D. W. (1985). Mental health computing in the 1980s: Clinical applications. *Computers in Human Services, 1*(2), 1-31.

Hedrick, T. E. (1988). The interaction of politics and evaluation. *Evaluation Practice, 9*(3), 5-14.

Herman, J. L., Morris, L. L., & Fitz-Gibbon, C. T. (1987). *Evaluator's handbook*. Newbury Park, CA: Sage.

Heying, K. (1985). Family based in-home services for the severely emotionally disturbed child. *Child Welfare, 64*, 519-527.

Hinckley, E. C. (1984). Homebuilders: The Maine experience. *Children Today, 13*(5), 14-17.

Hinckley, E. C., & Ellis, W. F. (1985). An effective alternative to residential placement: Home-based services. *Journal of Clinical Child Psychology, 14*, 209-213.

Hutchinson, J. R. (1983). *Family-centered social services: A model for child welfare agencies*. Iowa City: University of Iowa, School of Social Work, National Resource Center on Family Based Services.

Hutchinson, J. R., & Nelson, K. E. (1985). How public agencies can provide family-centered services. *Social Casework, 66*, 367-371.

Jacobs, F. H. (1988). The five-tiered approach to evaluation: Context and implementation. In H. B. Weiss & F. H. Jacobs (Eds.), *Evaluating family programs* (pp. 37-68). Hawthorne, NY: Aldine.

Jayaratne, S., & Chess, W. A. (1984). Job satisfaction, burnout, and turnover: A national study. *Social Work, 29*, 448-453.

Jones, M. A., Magura, S., & Shyne, A. W. (1981). Effective practice with families in protective and preventive services: What works? *Child Welfare, 60*, 67-80.

Landsman, M. (1985). *Evaluation of fourteen child placement prevention projects in Wisconsin 1983-1985*. Iowa City: University of Iowa, School of Social Work, National Resource Center on Family Based Services.

Lauffer, A. (1984). *Understanding your social agency* (2nd ed.). Beverly Hills, CA: Sage.

Laughlin, J., & Weiss, M. (1981). News and views: An outpatient milieu therapy approach to treatment of child abuse and neglect problems. *Social Casework, 62*, 106-109.

Leeds, S. (1984). *Evaluation of Nebraska's intensive services project*. Iowa City: University of Iowa, School of Social Work, National Resource Center on Family Based Services.

Leeds, S. (1987). *Services to promote family stability and prevent foster care placement: Summary of findings*. Iowa City: University of Iowa, School of Social Work, National Resource Center on Family Based Services (Conducted in conjunction with the New Jersey Division of Youth and Family Services, Bureau of Research.)

Manning, P. K. (1982). Qualitative methods. In R. Smith (Ed.), *Handbook of social science methods* (pp. 1-28). Cambridge, MA: Ballinger.

Marshall, C., & Rossman, G. B. (1989). *Designing qualitative research*. Newbury Park, CA: Sage.

Maslach, C., & Jackson, S. E. (1981). *Human services survey* (research ed.). Palo Alto, CA: Consulting Psychologists.

Moos, R. H. (1988). Assessing the program environment: Implications for program evaluation and design. In J. K. Conrad & C. Roberts-Gray (Eds.), *Evaluating program environments* (pp. 7-23). Potomac, MD: American Evaluation Association.

Morell, J. A. (1982). Evaluation in prevention: Implications from a general model. *Prevention in Human Services, 1*, 7-40.

Nelson, K. E., Emlen, A., Hutchinson, J. R., & Landsman, M. J. (1988). *Factors contributing to success and failure in family-based child welfare services: Final report.* Iowa City: University of Iowa, School of Social Work, National Resource Center on Family Based Services.

Nelson, K. E., Landsman, M. J., & Deutelbaum, W. (1990). Three models of family-centered placement prevention services. *Child Welfare, 69*(1), 3-21.

Neugeborn, B. (1985). *Organization, policy and practice in the human services.* New York: Longman.

Patton, M. Q. (1980). *Qualitative evaluation methods.* Beverly Hills, CA: Sage.

Pecora, P. J., Delewski, C., Booth, C., Haapala, D., & Kinney, J. (1985). Home-based, family-centered services: The impact of training on worker attitudes. *Child Welfare, 64*, 529-540.

Pecora, P. J., Fraser, M. W., Haapala, D. A., & Bartlome, J. A. (1987). *Defining family preservation services: Three intensive home-based treatment programs* (Report No. 1). Salt Lake City: University of Utah, Social Research Institute.

Peterson, K. A., & Bickman, L. (1988). Program personnel: The missing ingredient in describing the program environment. In J. K. Conrad & C. Roberts-Gray (Eds.), *Evaluating program environments* (pp. 83-92). Potomac, MD: American Evaluation Association.

Roberts-Gray, C., & Scheirer, M. A. (1988). Checking the congruence between a program and its organizational environment. In J. K. Conrad & C. Roberts-Gray (Eds.), *Evaluating program environments* (pp. 63-82). Potomac, MD: American Evaluation Association.

Rossi, P. H., & Wright, S. R. (1977). Evaluation research: An assessment of theory, practice, and politics. *Evaluation Quarterly, 1*, 5-51.

Rzepnicki, T. L. (1987). Recidivism of foster children returned to their own home: A review and new directions for research. *Social Service Review, 61*, 56-70.

Showell, W., Hartley, R., & Allen, M. (1988). *Outcomes of Oregon's family therapy programs: A descriptive study of 999 families.* Salem: Oregon Department of Human Resources, Children's Services Division.

Sorensen, J. E., & Elpers, J. R. (1978). Developing information systems for human service organizations. In C. C. Attkisson, W. A. Hargreaves, M. J. Horowitz, & J. E. Sorensen (Eds.), *Evaluation of human service programs* (pp. 127-172). New York: Academic Press.

Taylor, J. B. (1981). *Using microcomputers in social agencies.* Beverly Hills, CA: Sage.

Tripodi, T., Fellin, P., & Epstein, I. (1978). *Differential social program evaluation.* Itasca, IL: F. E. Peacock.

Van Maanen, J. (1979). The process of program evaluation. *Grantsmanship Center News, 6*(27), 29-74.

Wildavsky, A. (1972). The self-evaluating organization. *Public Administration Review, 32*, 509-520.

*4*

# *Service Inputs and Outputs*

## CAROL L. PEARSON

One of the hallmarks of family preservation models is the wide variety of services that workers use to achieve program goals. Because of this variety and the structural differences in service delivery across programs, evaluators need a common, coherent framework for measurement, data collection, and subsequent analysis. This chapter presents a service delivery taxonomy, various measurement and data collection methods, and options for analyzing service delivery strategies.

## *Toward a Service Delivery Taxonomy*

The need for a common service taxonomy can best be understood through a description of the family preservation services model. The first section of this chapter will focus on the variety of services that might be used within a family preservation program or in other family-based service programs.

### Intake and Referral

Referrals to a family preservation program may come from a variety of sources, such as public agencies, schools, hospitals, police, and courts. Once a case is accepted, attempts at face-to-face contact are usually made within 24 hours, but, in some instances, there may be a delay in meeting the family.

Evaluators must define the procedures and timing of the referral process. Although many programs initiate contact within 24 hours, other public agency programs, such as the Maryland Intensive Family Services Program, may take as long as five days before initial family contact (Maryland Department of Human Resources, 1987).

## Initial Family Contact

Family preservation services models have a common goal of smooth family functioning with a minimum of formal outside intervention (Hutchinson, Lloyd, Landsman, Nelson, & Bryce, 1983; Maryland Department of Human Resources, 1987). Building on family strengths is crucial. At the time of referral and before the initial contact, the program staff may seek information about problem areas and evidence of family competence. Pivotal family members are identified at least tentatively by the end of the initial contact.

At the first meeting, the program staff and, ideally, all family members who significantly affect family functioning meet in the home. Program staff explain the services to the family, emphasizing the following:

- the commitment to family preservation and the family as a key resource for change
- the time-limited, intensive nature of the service
- the fact that treatment goals are determined by the family
- the commitment to an agreed-upon action plan

During the first meeting, all family members are encouraged to offer their perspectives and voice their concerns about the family's problems, including the type of change that is necessary. This approach enables staff to observe the family's interaction. In addition, the family learns about staff availability and how to contact staff members. Most programs have 24-hour staff available for maximum family access.

Although assessment may stretch over several contacts, an initial plan of action is usually devised and implemented by the end of the first meeting. For example, the staff may arrange for supportive services such as money to cover payment of utility bills or purchase of diapers. The action plan may include tasks such as a parent agreeing to play for 10 minutes a day with a neglected child or a parent calling the school for information about a child. The initial plan usually addresses the issues of abuse, neglect, and alcoholism or other substance abuse.

### Intensity of Contact and Staffing

In addition to responding to calls from families, therapists often schedule meetings to continue assessment, review progress on the plan, and take further concrete steps toward change. In the first two weeks and throughout treatment, the evaluator should consider it important to monitor in-person contact in the home or phone contact with family members, in order to measure intensity of contact.

Family preservation models vary widely in terms of length of service delivery and staffing arrangements. It is important for the evaluator to clarify the average length service delivery time and who is offering services in a given program. Most programs are short term, but they may vary from six weeks to six months in duration.

In the Maryland Intensive Family Service Program, the worker, aide, and supervisor coordinate their efforts closely, determining the treatment plan, role assignments, and any other general tasks related to a case (Maryland Department of Human Resources, 1987). However, many family preservation programs do not use teams. In these programs, one social worker has the primary responsibility for providing the family with a wide range of services. Smaller caseloads enable workers to provide a variety of services.

Although the worker receives supervisory consultation, contact between the family and other program staff is minimal or non-existent.

## Treatment Strategies

Most family preservation programs incorporate a detailed and/or focused assessment into the treatment plan. Successful treatment planning requires that staff have at least several family and community contacts to understand the ecosystem in which the family lives (Hartman, 1978).

Depending on the program's theoretical approach, different techniques and strategies may be used to assess family functioning and to devise intervention strategies. Some programs use a social learning approach that emphasizes teaching skills to families in such areas as communication, child discipline, or household management. For programs that emphasize a family systems approach, the staff must understand the sequence of behaviors in which the primary problem is embedded and how the family perpetuates the problem. Observing and analyzing these sequences and then devising interventions for family members to respond differently are thought to be critical to the treatment process. For example, a 10-year-old habitually "goes out of control" and the mother feels "helpless." A treatment goal may be stated as follows: to create a situation in which the mother feels able to respond adequately or the child does not "go out of control."

Some programs have staff use "ecomaps" (Hartman, 1978), either with the family or upon returning to the office, to diagram how the family interacts with extended family, friends, schools, churches, and neighborhood groups, as well as with social service agencies. This exercise identifies resource linkages that can already be built upon, existing linkages that need facilitation, and absent linkages that must be created.

Planning for services involves synthesizing the assessment data and the priorities for change as perceived by the program staff and the family. In most family preservation programs, the service agreement includes these priorities, clear behavioral objectives, time limits, role delineations, and a list of community resources that will be explored and, whenever feasible, used. Evaluators need to establish with program managers whether or not the service agreement is considered a major service delivery component, and, if so, usage can be measured.

Flexible home-based practice requires that the staff use a combination of techniques, modalities, and approaches tailored to each family. A few of these are highlighted below.

*Family therapy/counseling.* Most programs find that a family meeting with most or all immediate family members is an effective way to begin involvement with the family. The staff observe family members' behavior together, support the adults, and ensure that the children's thoughts are heard. Meetings give the staff the opportunity to model constructive behavior and establish communication rules.

A variety of family therapy techniques may be used. In Maryland, three techniques are commonly used. One technique is "reframing," which takes the form of challenging the family's negative views of itself and others by emphasizing what the staff see as strengths. Another technique, the use of "enactments," is based on the need of individuals actually to experience new behavior in order for change to occur. Enactments usually take the form of activities that the program staff devise to help the family experience new behavioral sequences in the home, such as supporting a mother in organizing and running a family meeting. The technique of using "directives" involves the development, by the project staff and the family, of assignments for the family to work on between meetings (Maryland Department of Human Resources, 1987).

In behavioral and social learning programs, assertiveness, conflict management, child discipline, and other skills may be taught at family therapy sessions. Actual behavior of individuals, family subunits, and the family as a whole is observed, and feedback is given to the family. "Active listening" is a technique used for clarifying problems and misunderstandings.

*Individual counseling.* Another modality often used in treatment of the family is that of individual in-home meetings with a specific family member. Such meetings provide extended attention and emotional nurturance to a given individual, such as an overwhelmed single parent, a fearful child, or an elderly grandmother. In these sessions, personal and historical information can be gathered, feelings explored, and new behaviors rehearsed. Individual therapy with a child may involve some play therapy to encourage the expression of feelings.

*Subsystem intervention.* Activities that focus on a subsystem in the family represent another important intervention modality. These activities may focus on parental skill building, problematic spousal interactions, or any other interactive problem within a family. One important subsystem focus of many programs is that of marital relations.

*Assessment of resource and other needs.* Many service plans also respond to the family's acute material needs. Some projects provide emergency funds to improve the family's physical well-being. Rental deposits, food, clothing, shelter, transportation, and/or furniture are subsidized on a limited basis, if no other resources are available. Another group of support services includes arranging for specific ancillary services such as day care, chores or cleaning, respite, legal services, or other specialized services. The extent to which these services are utilized is related to both family needs and program definition. Similarly, whether these services are seen as supports for a more self-sustaining family organization or as rewards for other behaviors varies with different program models.

*Family network mobilization.* This modality combines family therapy, group therapy, and community organization. Network meetings, often at the family's home, may include members of the immediate family, significant friends and neighbors, extended family, coworkers, ministers, and other professionals. The focus is usually on a specific family problem, bringing together the family's support network to arrive at a coordinated effort to solve the problem.

*Family-community agency coordination.* This modality focuses on improving the linkage between the family and a particular agency. A typical example is consultation with school personnel and parents on children's school attendance and performance. The staff's role may be to help interrupt mutual blaming sequences, to promote listening, or to provide additional technical expertise in addressing school-related problems.

*Other service activities.* In addition to the services described above, family preservation workers also conduct other activities that affect the services they provide. Service coordination may require a substantial amount of time, as workers act as advocates, coordinators, and service brokers. Furthermore, to widen perspective, individualize strategies, and replenish the staff's technical and emotional resources, the supervisory consultation is another important activity. The frequency or intensity of these meetings may be an important factor in service effectiveness (Pearson & King, 1987).

## A Proposed Taxonomy

The preceding description of typical family preservation services underscores the need to develop a common, coherent framework within which evaluators can more readily understand the services. Such a framework will help evaluators describe and measure within and among programs who does what, when, where, and why, and how service may relate to outcome.

The following taxonomy divides into three general categories the services included in all family preservation models:

- *Clinical services* typically encompass the various professional social work treatment interventions that the staff provide directly during contacts with the family.
- *Concrete and support services* include a broad range of resources. They are usually closely related to material needs, highly specific, and not characterized by professional intervention. The worker generally acts as an intermediary.

**Table 4.1** Examples of Services Offered

| Clinical Services | Concrete and Support Services | Case Management Services |
|---|---|---|
| crisis intervention | food | case assessment |
| family therapy | clothing | case planning |
| group counseling | housing | case plan recording |
| marital therapy | household items | case supervision |
| individual counseling | utility payments | collateral coordination |
| drug/alcohol abuse | transportation | follow-ups |
| counseling | health care | |
| play therapy | family planning | |
| | child care | |
| | parenting classes | |
| | vocational training | |
| | financial management | |
| | legal assistance | |

- *Case management services* include primarily administrative tasks. These services typically are not sustained but periodic, and require no family contact.

Examples of each type of service are depicted in Table 4.1.

After the definition of a basic taxonomy, the evaluator may subdivide categories of services according to the interest of the program evaluation. For example, a similar taxonomy of service is being tested in the evaluation of family preservation services in Connecticut. This taxonomy is presented in Figure 4.1 (Y.-Y. Yuan, personal communication, 1988).

### *Measurement/Data Collection Issues*

One of the most difficult issues regarding clinical service measurement is that of arriving at a clear, agreed-upon definition of the service. Definitions depend on what questions are being asked. For example, are program analysts interested in which clinical service

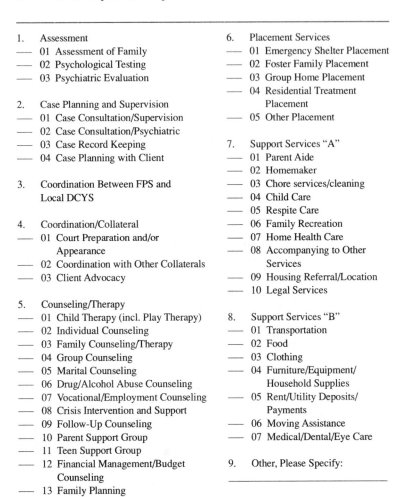

1.    Assessment
——  01  Assessment of Family
——  02  Psychological Testing
——  03  Psychiatric Evaluation

2.    Case Planning and Supervision
——  01  Case Consultation/Supervision
——  02  Case Consultation/Psychiatric
——  03  Case Record Keeping
——  04  Case Planning with Client

3.    Coordination Between FPS and
      Local DCYS

4.    Coordination/Collateral
——  01  Court Preparation and/or
          Appearance
——  02  Coordination with Other Collaterals
——  03  Client Advocacy

5.    Counseling/Therapy
——  01  Child Therapy (incl. Play Therapy)
——  02  Individual Counseling
——  03  Family Counseling/Therapy
——  04  Group Counseling
——  05  Marital Counseling
——  06  Drug/Alcohol Abuse Counseling
——  07  Vocational/Employment Counseling
——  08  Crisis Intervention and Support
——  09  Follow-Up Counseling
——  10  Parent Support Group
——  11  Teen Support Group
——  12  Financial Management/Budget
          Counseling
——  13  Family Planning
——  14  Parental Skills Training

6.    Placement Services
——  01  Emergency Shelter Placement
——  02  Foster Family Placement
——  03  Group Home Placement
——  04  Residential Treatment
          Placement
——  05  Other Placement

7.    Support Services "A"
——  01  Parent Aide
——  02  Homemaker
——  03  Chore services/cleaning
——  04  Child Care
——  05  Respite Care
——  06  Family Recreation
——  07  Home Health Care
——  08  Accompanying to Other
          Services
——  09  Housing Referral/Location
——  10  Legal Services

8.    Support Services "B"
——  01  Transportation
——  02  Food
——  03  Clothing
——  04  Furniture/Equipment/
          Household Supplies
——  05  Rent/Utility Deposits/
          Payments
——  06  Moving Assistance
——  07  Medical/Dental/Eye Care

9.    Other, Please Specify:
      _____

**Figure 4.1.** Service Codes

modality or technique is generally used during a given family contact?

Techniques are often not behaviorally specific in their definitions, or may occur so often in any given context that they are generally best measured by scales. Scales have most commonly been employed to identify the importance of various attributes of family preservation programs, the frequency of various techniques, and worker preferences among intervention approaches.

For example, to specify the types of treatment and intervention techniques that workers used in the Hennepin County Intensive In-Home Services Program, detailed questionnaires were developed (AuClaire & Schwartz, 1986; Pecora, Delewski, Booth, Haapala, & Kinney, 1985). A total of 36 different techniques were described, all with origins in five different approaches to practice: client centered, behavioral, structural, cognitive, and problem solving. Workers were asked to rate the extent to which they used each technique, yielding results that supported the framework of practice (structural family therapy) from which the workers were operating.

Clear definition of the treatment model is especially important if the evaluator seeks to link specific clinical interventions and goals with service needs or client outcomes. The attempt to relate culturally sensitive services to client outcomes in the Illinois Preplacement Prevention Project for Black Families (Jeffries, 1987) failed primarily because these services were never clearly defined for measurement. The services were delivered in such a way that they could not be validated; the workers could not adequately describe the specific techniques utilized.

Most evaluations focus on the frequency of various services. The service measures employed most often are checklists completed by workers, indicating the frequency and type of service delivered to the particular family. It is important, however, to distinguish who delivers the service; in some programs, concrete services may be delivered by someone other than the lead worker, such as the case aide or team paraprofessional. Because staffing patterns may significantly affect the worker-family relationship and thus treatment outcomes and costs, it is also important to record on checklists who provides the service, whether the service is purchased, and how much is spent.

If the measurement instrument is a simple checklist that workers can update frequently throughout the month as part of ongoing service recording in the case record, the evaluator will more likely obtain useful and complete information. In the Maryland Intensive Family Services Project (Pearson & King, 1987), the monthly service provision checklist was on a multicopy, no-carbon form, so that as soon as workers completed their case-specific recording for the month, one copy could be submitted to the supervisor, one dispatched to the evaluator, and one left in the case record as an essential part of case recording. This particular instrument identified the type of service, its frequency, whether it was purchased, and its cost. In this evaluation, the specificity of clinical techniques was not critical to assessing program effectiveness.

**Measurement of Case Management Services**

Structural service delivery components can be measured in a variety of ways discussed below. It is important for the evaluator to define these structural elements in order to evaluate their contribution to program effectiveness.

*Staff accessibility.* An important component of many family preservation programs is the staff's accessibility to the family. Some programs provide 24-hour coverage; answering services, backup workers, and staff coverage on evenings and weekends are features of other service strategies. The frequency and timing of the use of such emergency services, by whom, and for what purposes must be quantified to make possible the evaluation of the influence of accessibility on outcomes. Many programs cannot afford to offer such services. The correlation of 24-hour accessibility with the outcome of placement prevention has yet to be determined.

*Case assignment and referral.* Although the relationship between response time and family preservation unit effectiveness remains unsettled empirically, crisis theory states that families are most amenable to change while they are in a state of crisis and "normal" coping mechanisms for dysfunctional situations are not working (Rapoport, 1970). If response time is substantial, family preservation units may be less successful (Pecora, Fraser, Haapala, &

Bartlome, 1987). This variable should be an essential component of case recording, providing useful feedback for both program monitoring and evaluation.

*Contact patterns.* The response time issue underscores the importance of workers' recording the dates, purposes, services, parties, locations, and durations involved in any family contact over the service delivery term. Workers keeping a log on these variables as part of the case record-keeping process can be extremely useful to workers, supervisors, and evaluators. As mentioned in Chapter 3, the effectiveness of various staffing patterns is still unclear. What interventions, delivered by whom, work under what conditions? Use of a multicopy no-carbon form can ease dissemination of the information to all interested parties (Pearson & King, 1987). These data can reveal the staffing pattern for home visits and can make it possible for the researcher to measure the amount of time spent in the home against that spent making contacts on the telephone or in the office. Contacts usually vary among families, and home contacts have been found to be highly related to outcome (Fanshel & Shinn, 1978.)

A measure of total hours of contact is important in comparing program models, but may be less useful than the pattern of contacts over time when assessing individual outcomes. For example, how much worker contact do clients receive during the first one or two weeks of service? Contacts may be most frequent at the initiation of service and then taper off. These data are necessary to determine the intensity of the services, particularly during the initial crisis period. Records of the total number of home, office, other in-person, and phone contacts provide an even clearer indication of service intensity.

The average length of time in days is a common measure of service duration. Most family preservation programs are time limited or short term. Programs vary in length from one to six months' average duration. Documentation of the date of referral, first contact, last contact, and final closing is important in measuring the average length of time a case is served in these programs. If there is some kind of assessment period or intensive follow-up period, a record of this time should be added or at least identified as a related service period.

Length of service may be related to a program's policies and procedures. There may be a formal time limit on service length or a periodic review process that encourages termination within a specific time frame. It is particularly important to try to assess the relationship of these policy constraints to case outcome, so that their impact on service effectiveness can be understood.

*Caseload size.* Caseload size, treatment length, and service intensity are interrelated. The average number of families a team serves should therefore be tracked regularly. Caseload size may vary with service delivery stage. New referrals, for example, may be more time-consuming for the worker than cases receiving follow-up services. Generally, programs having more frequent contact over a shorter period of time have smaller caseloads, sometimes only two cases per worker. Documentation of caseload size on monthly monitoring forms is a simple, informative way to compare programs.

*Termination.* How and when the family preservation services are terminated and what happens to the family afterward have important outcome implications. Has the family become dependent on the services? Does termination occur within the time frame of the treatment model? The family is usually connected with outside or community services. What services does the family continue to use and from whom? Does the family preservation unit provide any formalized follow-up or contact with the family after service termination? Each of these activities may vary depending on the program and the family. It is important to allow for measurement of posttermination activities.

## Conclusion

Measurement of service delivery components is critical to program monitoring and evaluation. In examining measures of service components across programs, there is little consistency among the instruments employed. Most instruments seem to be program-specific creations. The important point, however, is that across all programs there should be a definite emphasis on record-keeping and other accountability devices, whether for ongoing program monitoring or evaluation. Keeping records on service delivery is vital to the success of the service intervention.

Documentation of what service was delivered to whom, under what conditions, both within and across cases and programs, provides critical feedback at many different levels. For instance, the information is necessary for the case manager who is responsible for case planning and coordination of team efforts and services toward a particular goal. Additionally, supervisors must keep abreast of service information to provide workers with necessary support and feedback. Furthermore, data on service delivery across several families are informative to the program administrator, who, depending on the stage of program development, may want to adjust the program model accordingly.

The evaluator's challenge is to develop record-keeping instruments that provide not only answers to the evaluation questions but also useful, readily obtainable information for program practitioners. Usually, the extent to which the evaluator is involved in the initial program development influences the success of this endeavor.

Even if the evaluator is charged with the development of service evaluation measures separate from the ongoing record keeping done by the practitioners, involving the practitioners in the design and modification of the instrument can certainly enhance the validity and reliability of the instrument. Unless the evaluator has the luxury of a large budget and can hire research assistants for case record abstracting, the practitioners themselves are usually responsible for data collection. Evaluation instruments incorporated into the ongoing record-keeping activity in a case increase the timeliness with which information is recorded, lessen the paperwork burden for the practitioner, and improve the quality and usefulness of the information collected.

## *References*

AuClaire, P., & Schwartz, I. (1986). *An evaluation of the effectiveness of intensive home-based services as an alternative to placement for adolescents and their families.* Minneapolis: Hennepin County Community Services Department and University of Minnesota, Hubert H. Humphrey Institute of Public Affairs.

Fanshel, D., & Shinn, E. (1978). *Children in foster care: A longitudinal investigation.* New York: Columbia University Press.

Hartman, A. (1978). Diagrammatic assessment of family relationships. *Social Casework, 59*(8), 465-476.

Hutchinson, J., Lloyd, J., Landsman, M., Nelson, K., & Bryce, M. (1983). *Family-centered social services: A model for child welfare agencies.* Oakdale: University of Iowa, School of Social Work, National Resource Center on Family Based Services.

Jeffries, Y. (1987). *Illinois preplacement prevention project for Black families: Program evaluation.* Springfield: Illinois Department of Children and Family Services.

Maryland Department of Human Resources. (1987). *Intensive family services: A family preservation service delivery model.* Baltimore: Author.

Pearson, C., & King, P. (1987). *Intensive family services: Evaluation of foster care prevention in Maryland.* Baltimore: Maryland Department of Human Resources.

Pecora, P. J., Delewski, C., Booth, C., Haapala, D., & Kinney, J. (1985). Home-based, family-centered services: The impact of training on worker attitudes. *Child Welfare, 64,* 529-540.

Pecora, P. J., Fraser, M. W., Haapala, D. A., & Bartlome, J. A. (1987). *Defining family preservation services: Three intensive home-based treatment programs* (Report No. 1). Salt Lake City: University of Utah, Social Research Institute.

Rapoport, L. (1970). Crisis intervention as a mode of brief treatment. In H. Roberts & F. Nee (Eds.), *Theories of social casework.* Chicago: University of Chicago Press.

# 5

# *Program Outcome Measures*

## MARK FRASER

Do family preservation services work? What impact do they have on parents and children? The purpose of this chapter is to describe measures that may be used in assessing the impact or outcome of home-based family treatment.

In social science parlance, the assessment of outcome is consonant with showing that a program or service is "effective." Proving that services are effective, however, is a difficult task. One must show that clients change in desirable ways after receiving a service. Equally important, one must show that the changes that clients make are due to the program and not to other influences, such as the natural dissolution of a crisis, receiving help from distant relatives, or taking medications. To demonstrate that clients' changes are due to the program and the program alone, it is necessary to eliminate all explanations other than the desired one— that is, that the program was responsible for changes in parents' behavior, children's improved performance in the home or school, prevention of out-of-home placement, and the like.

A carefully developed research design is necessary to prove that a program is effective. Rigorous designs—especially those that employ random assignment of subjects to control and treatment

77

groups—eliminate alternative explanations. Because designs are being discussed in other chapters, they will not be discussed here. Rather, measurement of change in children, parents, and families will be the focus of this chapter. Measuring change is a decisive step in building an argument that a program is effective.

## Building a Conceptual Framework

When a service fails, it is rarely the case that the entire service is ineffective. Rather, a component of the service is often found to be inappropriate or poorly implemented. So, before entering into the challenging task of assessing outcomes, every evaluator should ask: What are the discrete elements of the treatment provided by the workers? These elements may include different kinds of skills training (e.g., parenting, problem solving, communications, conflict resolution), crisis intervention, counseling or therapy, child care, transportation, health care, school liaison, or relationship building.

By conceptualizing services as having multiple elements, we may link outcome measures to each element. Perhaps the most critical problem in the area of outcome assessment is the selection of measures that match program goals. Poorly selected measures may show a perfectly effective program to be ineffective. Because policymakers seldom are knowledgeable enough to assess the "fit" between program content and measures used in an evaluation, they tend to use evaluation findings as if the measures selected are valid indicators of program outcomes. Consequently, it is important to select measures that are directly related to the kinds of services provided.

An initial step in selecting outcome measures is the development of a clear conceptualization and specification of service elements. From that should flow the selection of measures. Outcome measures can be regarded as direct expressions of the goals of service when service has been partitioned into its salient elements.

## Selecting Appropriate Measures

The selection of measures to assess program outcomes should be based on several principles, as listed below.

*(1) Know your social and political goals.* To what uses will the data be put? Choose measures that will serve your social and political goals. If data are to be used with legislators, select measures that will influence them. For example, although measures of family functioning may be of great importance to clinicians, legislators will want to know the bottom line. Are kids safe in homes receiving in-home family-centered services? Are placements prevented? Is money saved?

*(2) Select measures appropriate to your program's stage of development.* Newly formed programs should rarely conduct outcome evaluations. For them, it is usually far more fruitful to fine-tune the treatment model by developing a good conceptual framework and then to assess program processes, that is, to measure the amount and characteristics of services provided, to examine services element by element, and to develop a stable, well-trained staff.

*(3) Select proxy measures for global program goals.* Some program goals—for example, strengthening families—may be difficult to measure. Such goals are hard to concretize because they are theoretical concepts that have broad public appeal. But in practice, they have vague or multiple meanings. In such cases, measure proxies for a global treatment goal. For example, one might ask parents to rate the frequency and seriousness of the problems that they are having with their children. The sum total of scores (weighted by seriousness) across a variety of family problems can be used as an indicator of the strength that families have in meeting the day-to-day challenges of child care.

In the same vein, variables that are causally related to a global goal may be measured. For example, if a program goal is to prevent delinquency, one might attempt to measure parent-child attachment, school performance, and peer associations—all measures that have been shown to be predictive of delinquency.

*(4) Use multiple indicators.* Attempt to measure an important goal at least two different ways. If out-of-home placement is selected as an outcome measure, use both self-reports from parents and official reports. Official reports such as purchase of service fiscal records or other case management information system data may be quite accurate in capturing information on foster care and group home placements. Placements in psychiatric facilities, drug treatment communities, and youth correction centers may not be available from the same source. Moreover, official reports rarely contain information on private placements, children who run away from home, and informal placements with neighbors or relatives. This information is largely procured through the self-reports of parents. Only through the use of multiple indicators can such descriptive and precise data be gathered on these types of family outcomes.

*(5) Use proximal and distal measures.* The terms *proximal* and *distal* refer to the conceptual closeness of an outcome measure to program activities. Staff in family-centered home-based service programs often attempt to change patterns of functioning in families. Helping families make such changes is a common treatment goal. When it is a goal of treatment, measures of family functioning can be considered "proximally tied" to program activities, and they should be used to assess program outcomes. In contrast, distal outcomes tend to be less closely tied to specific program activities. They may be goals—such as the prevention of placement—that staff hope are the outcome of an entire constellation of services and treatment activities.

Distal outcomes include the long-term results of treatment. That is, over a period of time outcome evaluators seek to describe what happens to clients who received services. Many family preservation programs have used out-of-home placement as a distal outcome (see, e.g., Reid, Kagan, & Schlosberg, 1988). Of course, as the period between the end of service and the point of assessment becomes greater, it becomes more and more difficult to attribute observed changes in clients directly to a specific program. There are a lot of influences in clients' lives, and a specific program is only one of them.

Distal outcomes also may include impacts on other programs, the service network, and third parties such as policymakers. Family preservation services are unique, and they may radically alter the service system network. They may affect the job descriptions of Child Protective Services workers. They may affect the attitudes of legislators. They may affect the media. They may change the criteria that judges use to place children in foster or group care. Although "systemic" impacts are rarely measured, they are important distal program effects.

*(6) Track clients after the termination of services.* Family preservation programs are expected to have an effect both during and after the provision of services. But how long after the termination of services can we reasonably expect services to have an effect? After all, human behavior is complex and many families lead stressful lives.

There are no clear guidelines for the length of follow-up. Some studies have used a period as short as 3 months; others have used as much as a 12-month period. Follow-up is complicated by the mobility of many clients. Families move around, and it is difficult to keep track of them. On the other hand, some studies have been successful in tracking down better than 90% of client families one year after the termination of treatment (see, e.g., Fraser, Pecora, & Haapala, 1988). At a minimum, most family preservation programs will be expected to keep track of child placements for 6 months after the close of treatment; as discussed below, this is a complicated task.

## Measures for
## Family Preservation Services Programs

In the following sections, a variety of measures of both proximal and distal program outcomes are discussed. Not intended to be an exhaustive list, the measures and instruments discussed in this chapter were selected because they have been used successfully in evaluating family preservation programs across the nation, and because their use presents problems that workers must face and resolve when they attempt to describe program outcomes. In this latter sense, they are included because they are exemplary of problems that may be encountered. In determining what measures to use, it may be helpful to consider the issues discussed here in relation to the key elements of the program. Some of the measures may be adopted, while others will not be appropriate. The researcher should be selective and adopt only measures that are directly related to specific program goals. Tailoring the selection of measures to program needs is fundamental to the strategic use of evaluation information.

## Assessing Treatment Processes

The degree to which a program is successful in delivering a service as it was conceptualized is the first global outcome measure that should be considered by new or restructured programs. Measures of the nature of services provided to clients may be related to other outcome measures. For example, in a program that emphasizes parenting training, one can examine the relationship between changes in child functioning and hours of parenting training received by clients. Such information is useful to staff and supervisors as services are developed and refined. Measurements of service activities have been discussed in Chapter 4.

## Assessing Proximal Outcomes in Parents and Children

Outcome measures that are closely tied to service activities—that is, proximal outcomes—are used typically to measure changes in clients' attitudes, feelings, skills, and behaviors. The measures discussed below may be used at intake and again at the close of services. By comparing the differences between pre- and posttreatment scores, it is possible to compute "change scores" that represent gains or losses that are caused by treatment or, lacking a rigorous evaluation design, that are associated with receiving home-based services.

*The Child Well-Being Scales.* The Child Well-Being Scales (CWBS) were designed to measure family, parent, and child problems of the sort typically encountered by child protection workers. Filled out by the worker, the instrument consists of fully anchored rating scales that describe parenting role performance, familial capacities, child role performance, and child capacities (Magura & Moses, 1986).

The CWBS quantify 43 different dimensions of the physical, psychological, and social needs of children. They include items that describe physical health care, nutrition, clothing, household furnishings, overcrowding, sanitation, parental supervision of young children, consistency of discipline, abusive discipline, deprivation of food/water, and measures of child behavior such as academic performance, school attendance, and misconduct.

For each item, there are three to six response categories, and response categories are completely defined in order to increase reliability. For example, the scale describing "physical safety in the home" has five response levels:

(1) Safe: There are no obviously hazardous conditions in the home.
(2) Somewhat safe: There are one or two hazardous conditions in the home, but the child has not sustained injury as a result.
(3) Moderately unsafe: There are many hazardous conditions in the home, but the child has not sustained injury as a result.
(4) Seriously unsafe: There are one or two hazardous conditions in the home, and the child has sustained a physical injury requiring medical treatment as a result.
(5) Severely unsafe: There are many obviously hazardous conditions in the home, and the child has sustained a physical injury requiring medical treatment as a result.

The scoring of the CWBS makes it possible to assess the well-being of a single family or a child in a family. Seriousness "weights" are assigned to each level of each scale, permitting estimation of the relative contribution of each condition to the welfare of the child. Seriousness scores range from 100 (adequate) to 0 (most serious and completely inadequate) and were determined empirically (see Magura & Moses, 1986, pp. 157-166).

The Child Well-Being Scales have acceptable psychometric properties and appear particularly well suited to family preservation programs that have a high proportion of child abuse/neglect clients. The use of seriousness scores to give differential weight to various items makes the CWBS one of the more precise and useful instruments in the field.

*The Family Risk Scales*. Developed as a part of a study of child placement preventive services in New York State, the Family Risk Scales (FRS) were designed to assess a child's risk of entry into foster care (Magura & Moses, 1986). Scale items are fully anchored and were selected because it was believed that they were predictive of out-of-home placement (Magura, Moses, & Jones, 1987).

The FRS contain 26 items, each of which has four to six response categories. All response categories are based on an adequate to inadequate performance continuum. For example, "parental supervision of children under age 10" has four response codes: 1 = "adequate supervision and substitute care"; 2 = "some difficulties with supervising children . . . but no identifiable danger"; 3 = "considerable difficulties with supervision . . . leading to identifiable danger (but no harm or injury)"; 4 = "harm or injury resulting from improper supervision." Each response code is further defined in brief paragraphs that provide examples.

Each of the 26 items is designed to measure a different parent-related, child-related, or economic risk factor. Items cover habitability of the family residence, suitability of living conditions, financial problems, social support, parental health, parental mental health, parental substance abuse, parenting skill, use of physical punishment, use of verbal discipline, sexual abuse of child, child's health, child's mental health, child's school adjustment, delinquency, child's home-related behavior, and other risk indicators.

The breadth of the FRS is both an advantage and a disadvantage. On one hand, many behaviors and conditions are rated, making the instrument economical in the sense that a large number of variables are assessed with a very few measures. On the other hand, most of the risk factors are complex multidimensional phenomena that should properly be assessed by a series of questions. The FRS provide a global assessment of functioning, but programs that are funded to provide services to special populations—such as delinquent or substance-abusing youths and their families—might seek to augment these scales with more detailed assessments.

On balance, the scales are easy to use and constitute a significant contribution to the field. After initial training and practice, it takes workers about 20 minutes to fill out the FRS. Internal consistency scores (Cronbach's alpha) are acceptable, on the order of .80, and comparative data are available from a sample of 1,158 families (2,287 children) referred to preventive programs in New York City.

*The Family Adaptability and Cohesion Scales.* The Family Adaptability and Cohesion Scales (FACES III) were designed to measure family adaptability and cohesion. These scales form a self-report inventory, and family members over 12 years of age appear to be able to fill it out without trouble. It may be used to describe family functioning at the moment (real functioning) or family functioning in the ideal state (ideal functioning).

Based on the circumplex model of marital and family systems in which families may be classified into one of sixteen different types (Olson & Killorin, 1985), FACES III contains ten items that measure family adaptability and ten items that measure family cohesion. *Adaptability* refers to the capacity of a family to adjust to new conditions and includes such concepts as the nature of family leadership (authoritarian, equalitarian, erratic), discipline (strict, democratic, laissez-faire), use of negotiation, role sharing, and consistency of rules. *Cohesion* refers to the closeness—emotional bonding, family involvement, marital unity, parent-child coalitions, and boundaries—in a family. Adaptability is scored from low to high on a continuum with four anchors: rigid, structured, flexible, and chaotic. Cohesion is scored from low to high and has four different anchors: disengaged, separated, connected, and enmeshed. Sixteen family types are defined by cross-classifying the two variables. Olson, Portner, and Lavee (1985) have computed norms for each type of family and have conducted extensive analyses using FACES-derived measures.

Three FACES-related scale scores may be used. Adaptability and cohesion scores taken before and after treatment can be used to assess changes in family functioning during treatment. In addition, a distance-from-center score may be developed. Based on the circumplex model, adaptability and cohesion are not linear measures. Extreme scores at both ends of the adaptability (rigid and chaotic) and cohesion (disengaged and enmeshed) scales are considered dysfunctional. Mid-range scores (structured and flexible; separated and connected) are considered functional. Thus the degree to which a client's scores fall toward the upper and lower bounds indicates problematic behavior. The central hypothesis of the circumplex model is that families with balanced versus extreme scores perform better in treatment. The nonlinearity of these two scales restricts their analysis to cross-tabulations and other procedures that do not require an assumption of underlying ordinality.

To create a linear score of distance from the center, adaptability and cohesion scores are combined using a Euclidean transformation (for more information, see Olson et al., 1985, p. 34). This measure has acceptable properties for advanced statistical analyses and may be interpreted as an indicator of deviation from the balanced range. High scores indicate dysfunction and low scores indicate normative performance.

In the Family-Based Intensive Treatment Project, the factorial validity and internal consistency of the adaptability and cohesion indices for family preservation program clients were assessed. Factor solutions for cohesion were acceptable, but readers are cautioned that no acceptable factor solution was found for adaptability. Cronbach's alpha reliability at intake for cohesion was acceptable (alpha = .80), and it was moderately acceptable for adaptability (alpha = .64). The reliabilities of the cohesion and adaptability subscales at case termination (exit) were similar: alpha = .86 and alpha = .69, respectively (Fraser et al., 1988).

*The Family Environment Scale.* Developed by Rudolf Moos and Bernice Moos (1981), the Family Environment Scale (FES) contains 10 subscales that measure three underlying characteristics of families: relationships, personal growth, and system maintenance. Relationships are measured by subscales on cohesion, expressiveness, and conflict; personal growth or goal orientation, by subscales on independence, achievement orientation, intellectual-cultural orientation, active-recreational orientation, and moral-religious emphasis; and system maintenance, by subscales on organization and control.

Like the FACES III, the FES may be used in different ways. First, it can be used to describe existing family relationships by asking family members to fill it out describing what really happens in their homes (using the Real Form). Second, family members can be asked to describe their notions of an ideal family environment (on the Ideal Form). And third, family members can use it to describe their expectations for how the family environment might change given a major event, such as the placement of a child or successful family treatment (using the Expectations Form).

To my knowledge, the FES has not been used extensively in home-based programs. However, it has been shown to distinguish high-risk substance-abusing families from other distressed families, and thus it appears to be sensitive to the problems that characterize many families served in family preservation programs (Kumpfer, 1987; Kumpfer & DeMarsh, 1986). Based on data collected from a sample of 1,125 normal and 500 distressed families, norms are available for the FES. The test-retest reliabilities are acceptable, ranging from a low of .68 for independence to a high of .86 for cohesion (Moos & Moos, 1981, p. 5).

*The Child Behavior Checklist.* The Child Behavior Checklist (CBCL) was designed to record the problems and competencies of children between the ages of 4 and 16 (Achenbach & Edelbrock,

1983). The instrument may be filled out by parents, child caretakers, or teachers (it is slightly revised for teachers). It can be administered by an interviewer or may be used as a self-administered questionnaire. Factor-based scores for different dimensions of social competence and behavioral problems may be computed, and norms are available for boys and girls of different ages. The CBCL has been programmed for interactive entry by clients or staff, and so it is relatively easy to administer and to use in the development of child behavioral profiles.

To my knowledge, few family preservation programs have been able to assess child problems systematically from the perspective of parents, and this instrument appears to offer a clear and concise way to develop useful, comparable child profiles. Data are generated on children's activities (participation and skill in sports and nonsports activities), social involvement (number of friends, frequency of contact, and ability to get along with others), school performance (academic achievement, school-focused problems, and participation in special classes), and more than 100 specific problem behavior indicators (e.g., argues a lot, likes to be alone, sudden changes in mood or feelings). The instrument has acceptable test-retest and internal consistency reliabilities.

*Social support inventories.* In the past decade, the findings from numerous animal studies, analog experiments, and prospective surveys have suggested that social support is causally related to health maintenance, psychological well-being, and treatment prognosis (for a review, see Cohen & Wills, 1985). In particular, Wahler and his colleagues have found that failures in parenting training are correlated with "parental insularity," that is, lack of social support (see, e.g., Wahler, 1980).

Recently, Dumas, Wahler, and others have reported that socially isolated families are doubly at risk of treatment failure because they are not just isolated, they are embedded in coercive interactions with bill collectors, landlords, protective services workers, food stamp clerks, counselors, police, and other social control agents (Dumas, 1984; Dumas & Albin, 1986; Dumas & Wahler, 1983). The lack of social support appears to affect both the psychological and material resources that many families bring to bear in solving financial, housing, health, child-care, and other problems (see also Lewis & Fraser, 1987; Tracy & Whittaker, 1987). Thus insular families may be more likely to fail in home-based services.

Some programs explicitly attempt to alter the social support networks of clients. If social support is a critical factor in enabling families to respond to treatment, then assessing social support may be important. To measure social support, a variety of instruments are available (see Tardy, 1985). Developed by Barrera, Sandler, and Ramsay (1981), the Inventory of Socially Supportive Behaviors (ISSB) contains 40 items that focus on the frequency of occurrence of different kinds of supportive events (see also Barrera & Ainlay, 1983). In 1983, Robert Milardo revised the ISSB for use with distressed families and added items to measure aversive social interactions. At the same time, Milardo reduced the total number of items to 25 and expanded the response scale from five to seven categories: 1 = once a day or more; 2 = about every other day; 3 = about twice a week; 4 = about once a week; 5 = about once every two weeks; 6 = about once a month; and 7 = about once every two months.

Data on social support are usually collected just from parents, although older children may provide a different and valuable perspective on the social resources available to a family. Information about two general types of social support is gathered: (a) spousal (or cohabitant) social support and (b) extended family/nonkin (including neighbors, coworkers, acquaintances through organizations, and so on) support. Parents are asked to rate spousal support and extended family/nonkin support at the beginning of the program and once again at the end of services. Extended family and nonkin support is often defined so as to exclude activities that occur with spouses, live-in companions, children, or professional agency personnel such as mental health workers, social service workers, or homemakers.

To date, many scales measure only the frequency of specific supportive and nonsupportive events. Significantly, they do not appear to measure parents' views of the adequacy of their social support or their satisfaction with their social support.

Among families served by intensive in-home programs, three different types of social support appear to exist. Using the Milardo Scale, social support was measured in the Family-Based Intensive Treatment Project (Fraser et al., 1988) and three central elements of support were identified. The first element was called "empathetic friendship" and incorporated aspects of intimacy, unconditional acceptance, listening, and comfort. The second was called "aversion" and was characterized by coercive relationships involving blaming, criticism, and intrusion. The third element of social support was "coaching." It was defined by activities that involved exchanging information, teaching new skills, and receiving guidance, feedback, or advice. These three dimensions of social support among parents had excellent measurement properties, and changes in them were correlated with treatment outcomes. Such findings indicate that social support may mediate successful and unsuccessful outcomes in home-based services.

*Delinquency and substance abuse.* Delinquency and substance abuse are crucial social problems of our time, and changes in them may be used as measures of the impact of family preservation programs. Through peer groups and family members, many children are exposed to delinquency and the use of different kinds of psychoactive substances. Many are referred for noncompliance, status offenses, and delinquency. Some are described as "predelinquent," a term that refers to future risk of drug use, school dropout, delinquency, and other forms of rebellious behavior. Consequently, many programs target reducing delinquency and substance abuse as treatment goals. For such programs, it is appropriate to measure changes in delinquency and substance use.

Delinquency and substance abuse are illegal behaviors, and one might expect that self-reports of them would be biased. However, research has shown that self-reports from youths yield reliable and accurate information when confidentiality is guaranteed (Hindelang, Hirschi, & Weis, 1981). Thus perhaps the best way to estimate a youth's delinquency and drug involvement is to ask him or her specific questions about specific illegal acts.

The accuracy of self-reports drops off when sensitive words are used, and so the names of some offenses must be paraphrased (Elliott, Huizinga, & Ageton, 1985). For burglary, rather than asking, "Have you committed burglary?" it is better to ask, "In the last six months, have you broken into a building and taken something?" Similarly, for robbery, one might ask, "In the last X months, have you used a weapon to get something from someone?" Or for shoplifting, "In a store, have you taken things ($10 to $50) without paying?"

Assessment of substance abuse and use requires equal specificity, because it is necessary to find out about both the types and quantities of drugs being used (see, e.g., Johnston, O'Malley, & Bachman, 1985). Drug involvement ranges from experimentation with licit drugs (tobacco and alcohol) to regular use of illicit drugs such as cocaine and marijuana. And to separate what some might consider "normal" experimentation from deeper involvement, it is necessary to ask quite pointed questions, for example: "In the last 30 days, on how many occasions have you used marijuana?" or "Over the last month, on how many different occasions have you used alcohol? How many drinks do you usually have when you drink?"

In sum, in using self-report measures of illegal behaviors of youths, such as drug use, guarantees must be given that responses will be confidential and not subject to use in treatment. If a program is providing services under contract to a public agency, such issues as mandatory reporting must be clarified in advance of implementation of forms.

*School performance.* School is a major socializing institution for children, and school performance is predictive of delinquency, substance abuse, mental illness, and a variety of other problems (see, e.g., Hawkins, Lishner, & Catalano, 1985; Loeber, 1987). The children in many families receiving intensive family preservation services do poorly in school, and many workers attempt to help families by setting up home-school note systems (to increase communication between parents and teachers), encouraging parents to discuss school activities with their children, and defining contingencies (incentives and punishments) for school performance.

If improving school performance is a treatment goal, multiple measures of school performance can be collected. These include, but are not limited to, attendance, teacher ratings of classroom deportment, grade point average (in junior high and high school), attachment to teachers (or other adults in school), school friends, and attitude toward school. A growing body of research is showing that study habits and deportment in the very early grades are associated with subsequent problems in the community, and, in one recent evaluation of intensive in-home services, school involvement was correlated with service outcomes (Fraser et al., 1988).

Obtaining school data is not easy. Schools are approached regularly by researchers, and, in order to protect students and their families, school officials have developed formal procedures to screen all research requests. From the teacher through the principal and area supervisor to the district superintendent, every official must be briefed on the nature of the research tasks and given assurances that students' rights will not be violated. Although an evaluator may obtain district-level approval, the support of the local principal will be critical to the success or failure of his or her data collection effort. It is generally wise for the researcher to begin seeking support at the principal level and to work up and down the ladder from there.

Two kinds of school-based data can be obtained. First and easiest, official school records of attendance, deportment, and academic achievement may be opened to the evaluator. These are quite useful in themselves, for truancy, deportment, and GPA are major predictors of behavior and community adjustment. Second and far more difficult is the involvement of teachers in data collection. At the lower grade levels, teacher reports of classroom behavior appear to be major correlates of home-related behavior and subsequent behavior in the community (see, e.g., Farrington & Gunn, 1985; Farrington & Tarling, 1985; Loeber, 1987). When teachers are willing and able to participate in an evaluation, their information is extremely helpful in the assessment of outcomes of treatment.

*Consumer satisfaction.* Parents and children are the consumers of family preservation services, and their opinions about the impact of services are very important. Consumer satisfaction may be both a proximal and a distal outcome measure. Global reports of satisfaction may be biased by social desirability, that is, parents' desire to please the worker or to protect themselves from cuts in service that they may fear will result from giving negative reports. Consequently, confidentiality must be guaranteed and measures of satisfaction should be focused, specific to discrete elements of service. For example, former clients might be asked to assess the importance of the in-home provision of service, skill-building or training activities, and the degree to which workers were available to help solve family problems. Descriptive data recounting the elements of service that were most helpful and least helpful may be valuable in fine-tuning a program.

Open-ended questions—such as "What was the most helpful aspect of the program?"—yield rich and colorful information. They make evaluation information come alive in the words of clients. If a large number of clients are asked such questions, however, someone must take time to sort through responses carefully to identify common replies. Only through such "content analysis" is it possible to reduce individual responses to central themes that may be helpful in assessment and planning.

### Assessing Distal Outcomes: Child Placement

The literature contains remarkable assertions regarding the effectiveness of in-home care. Studies indicate that many programs have been successful in preventing out-of-home placement. Some programs have been reported to prevent placement in over 85% of the cases that complete treatment (Cantley & Plane, 1983; Halper & Jones, 1981; Lawder, Poulin, & Andrews, 1984; Leeds, 1984; Rosenberg, McTate, & Robinson, 1982).

However, the measures of success and failure used in most evaluations have been quite limited. In particular, no common measures other than child placement have been used, and child placement has been defined many different ways; the follow-up periods across which families have been monitored have also varied significantly. In some cases placement of a child with a relative has been defined as failure and in other cases as success; in still other studies, placement of a child in a nonrelative foster or group home has been the sole determinant of service failure, with children who were placed in shelter care or who ran away from home excluded from analyses. The lack of a consistent, comparable outcome measure seriously compromises the literature on intensive in-home services.

Out-of-home placement is commonly used as an outcome measure. As has already been indicated, it is an important measure from the standpoint of public policy, and it has many different facets that will be described below.

*Type of placement.* "Out-of-home placement" is a complex measure. One must define at the outset those classes of outcomes that will be considered to constitute service failure and those that will constitute service success. These outcomes include such conditions as living in the home, with relatives, with friends, in shelter care, in a foster home, in a group home, in residential treatment, in an inpatient psychiatric facility, and in a state hospital. But they also include such outcomes as joining the armed services (and leaving home for basic training), running away from home, being sent to a boarding school, or moving into an apartment (emancipation). Moreover, a definition of service failure that is based on family preservation should include guidelines as to the amount of time a child must be out of the home before service should be considered to have failed. Should service be declared to have failed because a child went to live with a friend for a few days or because he or she was placed in detention for a week? How much time out of the home warrants a declaration of service failure?

Two practical issues must be considered in defining those conditions that will constitute service failure. First, funding sources and different court jurisdictions may specify those conditions that must be defined as failure. Often a child must be absent from the home for at least 24 hours before he or she can be considered to be "missing." Sometimes courts use 72-hour "cooling off" placements to separate family members during the heat of conflict. Such therapeutic placements are rarely considered to constitute service failure. Sometimes funding agencies are interested primarily in out-of-home conditions that result in the expenditure of public funding for selected services such as foster care. In short, local considerations may lead to the specification of failure and success conditions.

Second, the exigencies of collecting certain kinds of data may affect whether an out-of-home condition can be included as an outcome measure. It is very difficult to gather data on out-of-home conditions that are not routinely tracked by management information systems. When a child leaves home to live with relatives, neighbors, or friends or when parents admit a child to a private treatment facility, the home is disturbed and, from a family preservation perspective, some would view service to have failed. But to collect such data is time-consuming. It usually requires follow-up interviews with parents, and programs rarely have the resources to keep track of former clients.

In sum, purposeful decisions should be made regarding those classes of outcomes that will meet the agency's needs in describing successful and unsuccessful service outcomes. The decision to use management information system data may be expedient, but it also leads to an outcome measure that may be quite restricted. On the other hand, the decision to conduct a client follow-up in order to gather detailed information on child outcomes requires substantial resources.

*Number of placements.* In the course of follow-up periods that approach one year, some children will experience not just one placement but two or more. Placement information should reflect the number of placements experienced over a set follow-up period and any trends in the order of placements, such as placements in increasingly restrictive environments.

*Restrictiveness of placement.* Although this measure is rarely used, placements may be scaled on the basis of restrictiveness. Shelter care, detention, receiving care, and other short-term substitute care services are clearly less restrictive than residential treatment, inpatient psychiatric care, and correctional confinement.

*Length of placement.* Length of stay in the family is an intuitively appealing measure that is appropriate when, in an evaluation study, all client families are tracked for an equal period of time following service intake (or termination). Length of stay may be computed across any time period that is equivalent for all sample subjects, and it represents all days in a follow-up period in which a child was in the home. All placements are counted. For example, the child who, in the course of one year, experienced four placements of 30 days each would have a score of 245 ($365 - [30 \times 4] = 245$).

This measure has at least two limitations. First, it is not valid when families do not have the same opportunity to fail—that is, when the length of time between the start of a tracking period and its end varies. To ensure comparability, the length of the follow-up period must be carefully maintained if this measure is to be used. Second, the measure does not indicate how soon after treatment failure occurs. The interval between the end of services and the date of placement may be important in indicating the relative strength of home-based services over time.

*Proportion of placement days used.* This measure standardizes out-of-home placement over differing periods of time. Although it is desirable to track families over comparable periods of time, funding cycles, demands from legislators, and evaluation time constraints sometimes make it impossible to do so. At first blush, this measure appears to solve the problem of incommensurable follow-up periods. Proportion of placement days used is computed by dividing the number of days in placement by the total number of days in which a child is available for home and out-of-home placement. For example, the child who in the course of a year has been out of the home for 100 days would have a score of .27 (100/365), and the child who was placed for 27 of 100 possible days would also have a score of .27. Such percentages have been used to compare differences between treatment and control groups (see, e.g., AuClaire & Schwartz, 1986, p. 49).

There is, however, a conceptual problem with this measure. Youths with very short follow-up periods may be assigned scores that are quite similar to youths who have been relatively successful in staying in their homes over long periods of time. A youth who experiences no placement in one month's time would receive the same score as a youth who remained continuously in his or her home for 18 months. Thus the measure seems to have "ceiling" effects in that differing degrees of success are poorly distinguished.

*Hazard rate for placement.* The amount of time that elapses between intake and placement or, in the event that no placement was made, between intake and the end of a follow-up period may also be used as a measure of outcome. This permits the calculation of a "hazard" rate for placement. The hazard rate is the probability that a child will be placed at time $t$, given that the child was at risk at time $t$. At any point during the follow-up period the risk of placement for each child may be expressed as a hazard rate or the odds of placement. For example, if out of a sample of 200 children, 20 are placed in the first week of treatment, the odds of placement are 20/200, or 1/10. In the second week, if 18 children are placed, then the odds of placement are 18/180 (or still 1/10) because the sample at risk decreased in size by 20, the number of children placed in the first week.

A hazard rate may be computed for each child at risk of placement for every day or week of risk. Overall, the hazard rate may change as a function of time. Hypothetically, one might posit that the risk of placement would be higher just after intake and treatment termination than during the course of treatment and during the months following treatment. The former are points in time when families are making major changes. The hazard rate also may be different for families with different characteristics. For example, the hazard rate may be higher for families with older as opposed to younger at-risk children. In sum, hazard rates may change as a function of time and explanatory variables such as client, treatment, and worker/system characteristics. (For additional information on this topic, see Allison, 1984.)

## *Conclusion*

In the emerging era of practitioner-directed evaluation, program directors and staff are likely to find themselves increasingly in the position of collecting data from clients. The purpose of this chapter has been to describe some of the measures that might be used in assessing the impact of home-based services programs. However, another purpose of the chapter has been to discuss a few basic rules for undertaking evaluations of family preservation programs, including (a) assessing program social and political goals; (b) selecting sensitive measures that match program efforts, stage of development, and structure; (c) using proxy measures for complex outcomes; (d) measuring important outcomes with at least two different indicators; (e) using proximal and distal outcome measures; and (f) tracking clients after the completion of treatment.

As opposed to research that is liberally funded by federal programs or foundations, agency-level evaluation is frequently poorly funded. It must be economical and strategic. It should be used to advance practice knowledge and to strengthen programs. Rarely will it be possible for a home-based service program to conduct an experimental study, but it is possible to conduct small studies of the results of treatment among former clients, and it is equally possible to collect process data to assess the "fit" between services actually delivered and those described in program materials.

In sum, assessing program outcomes has become necessary. Fiscal and legal accountability demand it. But I have tried to suggest here that the potential uses of data—if they are collected carefully—are far broader than accountability. In home-based service programs across the nation, data are used in long-range planning, clinical supervision, program development, and service advocacy.

The challenge to such programs is to collect the right data at the right time.

## References

Achenbach, T. M., & Edelbrock, C. (1983). *Manual for the Child Behavior Checklist and revised Child Behavior Profile.* Burlington, VT: University Associates in Psychiatry.

Allison, P. D. (1984). *Event history analysis: Regression for longitudinal event data.* Beverly Hills, CA: Sage.

AuClaire, P., & Schwartz, I. (1986). *An evaluation of the effectiveness of intensive home-based services as an alternative to placement for adolescents and their families.* Minneapolis: Hennepin County Community Services Department and University of Minnesota, Hubert H. Humphrey Institute of Public Affairs.

Barrera, M., Jr., & Ainlay, S. L. (1983). The structure of social support: A conceptual and empirical analysis. *Journal of Community Psychology, 11*, 133-143.

Barrera, M., Jr., Sandler, I. N., & Ramsay, T. B. (1981). Preliminary development of a scale of social support: Studies on college students. *American Journal of Community Psychology, 9*, 435-447.

Cantley, P. W., & Plane, M. B. (1983). *Facilitating family change: A look at four groups providing intensive in-home services.* Unpublished manuscript, Wisconsin Department of Health and Social Services, Madison.

Cohen, S., & Wills, T. A. (1985). Stress, social support, and the buffering hypothesis. *Psychological Bulletin, 98*, 310-357.

Dumas, J. E. (1984). Interactional correlates of treatment outcome in behavioral parenting training. *Journal of Consulting and Clinical Psychology, 52*(6), 946-954.

Dumas, J. E., & Albin, J. B. (1986). Parent training outcome: Does active parental involvement matter? *Behavioral Research and Therapy, 24*(2), 227-230.

Dumas, J. E., & Wahler, R. G. (1983). Predictors of treatment outcome in parent skills training: Mother insularity and socioeconomic disadvantage. *Behavior Assessment, 5*, 301-313.

Elliott, D. S., Huizinga, D., & Ageton, S. S. (1985). *Explaining delinquency and drug use.* Beverly Hills, CA: Sage.

Farrington, D. P., & Gunn, J. (1985). *Aggression and dangerousness.* New York: John Wiley.

Farrington, D. P., & Tarling, R. (1985). *Prediction in criminology.* Albany: State University of New York Press.

Fraser, M. F., Pecora, P. J., & Haapala, D. A. (1988). *Families in crisis: Final report on the family-based intensive treatment project.* Salt Lake City: University of Utah, Social Research Institute.

Halper, G., & Jones, M. A. (1981). *Serving families at risk of dissolution: Public preventive services in New York City.* New York: Human Resources Administration.

Hawkins, J. D., Lishner, D., & Catalano, R. F. (1985). Childhood predictors and the prevention of adolescent substance abuse. In C. L. Jones & R. J. Battjes (Eds.), *Etiology of drug abuse: Implication for prevention* (ADM 85-1335). Rockville, MD: National Institute on Drug Abuse.

Hindelang, M. J., Hirschi, T., & Weis, J. G. (1981). *Measuring delinquency.* Beverly Hills, CA: Sage.

Johnston, L. D., O'Malley, P. M., & Bachman, J. G. (1985). Use of licit and illicit drugs by America's high school students, 1975-1980. (DHHS Pub ADM 85-1394). U.S. Department of Health and Human Services, Alcohol, Drug Abuse, and Mental Health Administration. Rockville, MD: U.S. Government Printing Office.

Kumpfer, K. L. (1987). Etiology and prevention of vulnerability to chemical dependency in children of substance abusers. In B. S. Brown & A. R. Mills (Eds.), *Youth at high risk for substance abuse* (ADM 87-1537). Rockville, MD: National Institute on Drug Abuse.

Kumpfer, K. L., & DeMarsh, J. (1986). Family environmental and genetic influences on children's future chemical dependency. In S. Griswold-Ezekoye, K. L. Kumpfer, & W. J. Bukoski (Eds.), *Childhood and chemical abuse: Prevention and intervention.* New York: Haworth.

Lawder, E. A., Poulin, J. E., & Andrews, R. G. (1984). *Helping the multi-problem family: A study of services to children in their own homes (SCOH).* Philadelphia: Children's Aid Society of Pennsylvania.

Leeds, S. J. (1984). *Evaluation of Nebraska's intensive services project.* Unpublished manuscript, University of Iowa, National Resource Center on Family Based Services, Iowa City.

Lewis, R. E., & Fraser, M. (1987). Blending informal and formal helping networks in foster care. *Children and Youth Services Review, 9,* 153-169.

Loeber, R. (1987). The prevalence, correlates, and continuity of serious conduct problems in elementary school children. *Criminology, 25*(3), 615-642.

Magura, S., & Moses, B. S. (1986). *Outcome measures for child welfare services.* Washington, DC: Child Welfare League of America.

Magura, S., Moses, B. S., & Jones, M. A. (1987). *Assessing risk and measuring change in families: The Family Risk Scales.* Washington, DC: Child Welfare League of America.

Milardo, R. M. (1983). Social networks and pair relationships: A review of substantive and measurement issues. *Sociology and Social Research, 68*(1), 1-18.

Moos, R. H., & Moos, B. S. (1981). *Family Environment Scale manual.* Palo Alto, CA: Consulting Psychologists.

Olson, D. H., & Killorin, E. (1985). *Chemically dependent families and the circumplex model.* St. Paul: University of Minnesota, Family Social Science.

Olson, D. H., Portner, J., & Lavee, Y. (1985). *FACES III.* St. Paul: University of Minnesota, Family Social Science.

Pecora, P. J., Fraser, M. W., Haapala, D. A., & Bartlome, J. A. (1987). *Defining family preservation services: Three intensive home-based treatment programs* (Report No. 1). Salt Lake City: University of Utah, Social Research Institute.

Reid, W. J., Kagan, R. M., & Schlosberg, S. B. (1988). Prevention of placement: Critical factors in program success. *Child Welfare, 62*(1), 25-36.

Rosenberg, S. A., McTate, G. A., & Robinson, C. C. (1982). *Intensive services to families-at-risk project.* Unpublished manuscript, Nebraska Department of Public Welfare and University of Nebraska Medical Center, Omaha.

Tardy, C. (1985). Social support measurement. *American Journal of Community Psychology, 13*(2), 187-202.

Thompson, M. S. (1980). *Benefit-cost analysis for program evaluation.* Beverly Hills, CA: Sage.

Tracy, E. M., & Whittaker, J. K. (1987). The evidence base for social support interventions in child and family practice: Emerging issues for research and practice. *Children and Youth Services Review, 9,* 249-270.

Wahler, R. G. (1980). The insular mother: Her problem in parent treatment. *Journal of Applied Behavior Analysis, 13,* 207-219.

*6*

# Cost Analysis

## YING-YING T. YUAN

Significant savings in child welfare services have been reported as a result of providing family preservation services. In this chapter basic principles in analyzing service delivery costs from a programmatic perspective are reviewed, and issues in comparing costs among different programs are discussed.

In the previous chapters, issues regarding the analysis of the structure, services, and outcomes of family preservation services programs have been discussed. In this chapter a framework for analyzing the cost of providing such services is presented.

There are several reasons for the current interest in examining the cost of providing family preservation services. One is that large savings have been attributed to these programs. The state of Washington, for example, has reported savings of more than $17 million over a period of 12 years through utilization of the Homebuilders home-based program (Koshel & Kinney, 1986). An earlier study by Kinney, Godfrey, Haapala, and Madsen (1979) reported a sav-

AUTHOR'S NOTE: I would like to thank the following friends and colleagues for taking the time in their busy schedules to provide wise counsel during the preparation of this chapter: Virginia Banerjee, Ronald Davidson, David Knaggs, Walter R. McDonald, and Leon Robertson.

ings of $2,507 per child when the costs of intensive in-home services were compared to placement services.

The second reason is that state and county governments are picking up a greater share of social service costs and are looking for new approaches to structuring services and funding. A recent analysis by the National Conference of State Legislatures reported that in 16 states, the federal share of expenditures on child welfare services had decreased from 36% in 1981 to 28% in 1985 and that the state share had increased from 54% to 66% over the same period (Smith, 1986). Using estimates from the Children's Defense Fund, the author argues that "the costs of maintaining a child in foster care can be effectively reduced by shifting dollars and efforts toward prevention, family reunification and adoption." Given the variation in expenditures for placement services and preventive services throughout the nation (Collins, 1987), it is no wonder that legislators are interested in examining the potential cost savings specific to their own jurisdictions. Local communities, especially county-administered social services systems, are also concerned, as they are often asked to increase their share in the funding of placement services (Robison, 1987).

The third reason is that over the last several years cost-effectiveness analysis has been introduced as an important, if difficult, part of evaluation. The use of such methodologies in the fields of job training, community mental health, and other health-related areas has increased the interest in cost analysis.

## Types of Analyses

In a manual on analyzing costs in human service programs developed for the Office of Human Development Services, cost analysis is defined as "a uniform system for collecting, organizing and analyzing cost information" (Elliot & Forman, 1980). Cost analysis is described as a management tool that provides quantitative information for planning and controlling routine operations, long-range program planning and policymaking, and service and product costing. It can be used to compare costs among organizations that have similar functions, to determine appropriate allocation of funds, and/or to establish rates that realistically reimburse providers for the cost of services. Used in combination with other data on the outcomes and outputs of service delivery, cost data can be analyzed in order to provide information for planning service delivery improvements.

The detailed description of program costs is a necessary prerequisite of cost outcome and cost-effectiveness studies and therefore is of basic importance in program evaluation (Hagedorn, Beck, Neubert, & Werlin, 1976). It is clear that such descriptions are in themselves not program evaluation, but the analyses of the data generated by these descriptions are an integral part of a comprehensive evaluation approach and contribute significantly to a greater understanding of the value or worth of a particular service to the community.

Smith and Smith (1985) distinguish seven different types of cost studies conducted by state-level evaluation units:

- *single cost description:* describes the costs of a single existing program
- *cost feasibility analysis:* determines whether a planned program is affordable within the resources available
- *cost utility analysis:* compares the costs of a planned program with its estimated outcomes
- *single cost outcome description:* compares the costs with outcomes of a single existing program
- *multiple costs description:* compares the costs of two or more existing programs
- *cost-effectiveness analysis:* compares the costs of outcomes of two or more existing programs where outcomes are measured in test scores, ratings, and so forth
- *cost-benefit analysis:* compares the costs with outcomes of two or more existing programs where both outcomes and costs are measured in dollars

Cost analysis, as part of an evaluation of family preservation services, can be designed to address several of these issues:

- Single cost descriptions and multiple costs descriptions can be developed to report on the actual costs of services, including costs of service over time.
- Single cost outcome descriptions can be developed to compare costs with outcomes.
- Cost-effectiveness analyses can be conducted to compare costs of two or more programs with regard to outcomes, including preventing the need for other services, such as substitute care.

Each of these goals requires a different amount of data and a different type of analysis. Furthermore, each poses different problems for the evaluator and the program administrators, and requires different resources for completion.

## *Family Preservation Services*
## *Evaluation Objectives*

In determining the objective of the cost analysis, the audience for the study and the source of program funding should be considered. A single project funded by a foundation grant or through demonstration funds from a state agency may expect to serve a certain number of families. The detailed analysis of costs incurred in providing the service will be of relatively little interest except as an accountability function. An evaluator wishing to include some indication of cost of service might establish a simple figure by dividing the amount spent on salaries and fringe benefits by the number of clients served, or by dividing the total grant by the number of clients served. Although the result may be of limited utility for comparative purposes, a more detailed analysis of costs may not be required. Furthermore, a public agency may not wish to invest in a detailed analysis of costs if it is providing demonstration funds to a number of projects, since start-up activities could skew the analysis.

Detailed cost breakdowns are more important when the service will be institutionalized following a demonstration or test period.

If the service is to be provided by private agencies, determination of actual costs becomes relevant as a basis for setting reimbursement rates by the public agency (Richardson, 1981). If the service is to be provided by either public or private agencies, an analysis of the cost of service will assist in developing the implementation and budgetary plan. In undertaking a comparative cost analysis as part of the evaluation of several projects, or as a planning step, several complex issues will arise. Projects may vary with respect to budget categories, line item definitions, funding ceilings per category, and funding sources. Not only may the cost breakdowns differ by project, but the question of who is paying for what may also differ. Some programs may include expenses met by their endowments, while others may not. Some may use formulas that reduce overhead costs, while others may maximize overhead costs. Techniques for allocating costs will also affect the reported cost of service. Under such circumstances, determining cost of service by simply dividing the total project costs by the number of clients becomes a methodology with a problematic amount of variation. Thus, for evaluators charged with examining the cost-efficiency and/or -effectiveness of multiple projects, there is a need to establish a uniform method of examining project costs prior to comparing programs.

The first objective of an evaluator might be a further detailing of the costs of a program—that is, elaborating upon the descriptive reporting incurred during program development and implementation. For example, if an agency is planning on implementing family preservation services throughout the state, an evaluator may be asked to assist in the projection of start-up costs for each jurisdiction. Based upon an analysis of the utilization of resources by a number of earlier demonstration projects, some assistance may be able to be provided.

A second objective of an evaluator might be to compare the costs of different projects. For example, two demonstration projects have been funded. One project receives $300,000 per year to provide family preservation services; another receives $150,000 per year to provide similar services. In evaluating the cost of service, the evaluator will need to examine whether the projects are providing similar services at similar or dissimilar costs. An evaluator might also be involved in determining the refunding of programs based upon a comparison of the efficiency of each project. If one project receives greater funding and yet serves the same number of families as another project that receives less funding, a study of types of expenditures and types of services may explain the difference in cost.

A third objective might be to compare the costs of family preservation services to the costs of alternative programs. Measures of efficiency of service delivery may be developed based upon cost data and service outcome data. The earlier chapter on outcomes has indicated that there are many types of outcomes that might be researched as part of the evaluation of a preventive service. Given the range of outcomes that may be studied and the different accounting systems used, comparative cost analysis research is complicated.

This chapter presents some of the issues and options for describing costs of preventive services, comparing the costs of multiple family preservation services programs, and comparing family preservation services costs to placement costs. After a brief summary of the rudimentary aspects of cost accounting, issues of special concern to evaluators are identified and appropriate measures of unit costs are discussed. The final section presents types of comparisons that can be investigated and the use of such data for planning.

## *Describing the Cost of*
## *Family Preservation Services*

In considering the cost of providing family preservation services, the evaluator will need to gain an understanding of the foundation upon which analyses can be conducted. This section discusses the major categories of costs that are usually included in a cost analysis, and how these categories apply to family preservation services. The actual work of allocating costs is usually undertaken by an agency's accounting staff. The evaluator needs to review the products from the agency and to establish the comparability of the cost details from the various agencies. The following assumptions are made:

(1) The agency being studied has defined family preservation services as a cost center.
(2) The evaluator has the objective of comparing costs between different agencies or projects.
(3) The evaluator is examining the costs of services in the private sector and/or the public sector.

As in the situations discussed in earlier chapters, the roles of the evaluator and other agency personnel, in this case the accounting staff, are separate but related (see Hagedorn et al., 1976). When analyzing the cost of a particular service, the evaluator is dependent upon the accounting staff to make the necessary information available. If an agency does not structure its accounting system in terms of cost centers appropriate for the evaluator to analyze, there may be intrinsic difficulties in conducting an analysis. Agencies that have not recognized the service as a cost center may be unable to separate specific service costs from other agency costs.

Defining family preservation services as a cost center entails attributing direct costs and indirect costs. Direct costs include expenditures for personnel and other activities directly related to the program. Indirect costs, or support expenses, are those that are necessary for the functioning of the agency as a whole and indirectly for the program.

## Direct Costs

The largest category of direct costs usually consists of the salaries and fringe benefits of the professional and nonprofessional staff providing services or support work to the program. There are several ways of allocating these costs to the program:

(1) Some staff may work exclusively for the program. The salaries of these staff are automatically assigned to the program cost center.

(2) Some staff may contribute to several programs. Their salaries may be prorated across cost centers by recording in detail the time spent on this program and on others, by estimating the time spent, or by doing a periodic time study (see Hagedorn et al., 1976, for a review of these methods). In most family preservation programs, the caseworkers work exclusively for the program, while supervisors and managers may work for several programs. In addition, there may be outside consultants.

Other expenses commonly attributed as direct costs include telephone, postage, supplies, travel, publications, and equipment. Several lists of direct costs are available. Unfortunately, there is no single taxonomy for cost reporting being used by all agencies, although the guidelines of the United Way of America are often implemented. Most state and private agencies use their own set of line items and functional areas for defining costs. Jurisdictions may also vary as to the accounting methods. Cost accounting and accrual-based accounting are the methods most commonly used. Depending on the level of accuracy desired, the evaluator will need to be aware of these differences.

One list of direct costs that is familiar to a large number of agencies is that used by the U.S. Department of Health and Human Services (DHHS) in establishing contracts. The *Discretionary Grants Administration Manual* (U.S. DHSS, 1986) lists examples of allowable direct costs. Table 6.1 lists allowable and unallowable direct costs.

The *Discretionary Grants Administration Manual* leans toward including as much as is easily identifiable in direct cost categories. Thus it specifies that direct costs include those that "can be directly assigned to the project or activity relatively easily with a high degree of accuracy" and that indirect costs include those items that are not readily identifiable with a particular project or program, but are nevertheless necessary to the general operation of the organization, including such costs as operating and maintaining buildings, grounds, and equipment; depreciation; and administrative salaries. Prior to calculating indirect costs of a program, an agency might decide to include additional items in the direct pool. A list provided by the U.S. DHHS Office of Human Development Services (1986)

**Table 6.1** HDS List of Direct Cost Categories

| Most Common Allowable Categories | Most Common Unallowable Categories |
| --- | --- |
| advisory or policy council | advertising |
| alterations and renovations | bad debts |
| article page charges | construction |
| child-care costs | contingency fund reserves |
| consultant services | contributions and donations |
| educational/cultural activities | entertainment |
| equipment | fines and penalties |
| food services | fund-raising |
| fringe benefits | honoraria |
| indemnification | influencing legislation |
| motion picture production | interest costs |
| overtime pay | legal costs |
| publications | purchase of land or buildings |
| registration fees | |
| salaries and wages | |
| supplies | |
| travel | |

of costs that may be treated as either indirect or direct includes advertising, audits, bonding, books and periodicals, communication, depreciation or use charges, dues, equipment maintenance and repairs, insurance, legal costs, relocation, rental of equipment and facilities, taxes, and transportation of goods (pp. 3-1, 3-3).

**Indirect Costs**

As defined above, indirect costs are those expenses that cannot be directly ascribed to a particular program or project that delivers services. Indirect costs are more complicated than direct costs because they involve formulas that are established by each agency. When using cost data reported in project budgets, invoices, or agency accounts, an evaluator may find significant variation due to these formulas.

In many agencies indirect costs are directly attributed to support cost centers and then allocated to final cost centers. There are different methods of allocating these costs. Most common are formulas that redistribute the expenses of support cost centers to other cost centers. These formulas may be based on the actual amount of service provided or on a percentage allocation utilizing number of personnel or amount of space used. (The DHHS guidelines discussed above use a fixed ratio between indirect costs and a direct cost base composed of either direct salaries and wages or total direct costs excluding capital expenditure. For example, an agency will have an approved indirect cost rate that can be applied to all grants and contracts.) One approach to calculating indirect costs is to divide the project's total salary expenditures by the agency's total salary expenditures, and to use that ratio as the formula for allocating the project's share of the agency's total indirect costs. An alternative approach is to use the number of full-time personnel assigned to the project divided by the total number of full-time personnel in the agency as the formula for allocating the agency's indirect costs. Copeland and Iversen (1981) demonstrate that these two alternatives can have strikingly different results with regard to allocating general administrative costs.

In determining the method of allocating indirect costs, several factors may have influenced the decision of the agency. Under some funding regulations, indirect costs must be kept to a minimum; therefore an agency may have decided to maximize allowable direct costs. In other circumstances, the indirect percentage is not restricted, and there may be less incentive to maximize the direct costs categories.

If there is a ceiling on the allowable indirect cost rate, it can be advantageous for an agency to include as many items as possible in the direct costs categories. The agency's accountants may have determined the items to be included under direct costs. Before using the expenditures labeled as direct costs by a project or project(s) in understanding the costs of providing intensive in-home services, the evaluator will need to examine what is included in this classification. The evaluator may choose to separate personnel costs from other direct costs and establish the labor costs separately from all other expenses, regardless of whether these have been labeled direct or indirect costs. On the other hand, the evaluator may need to reconstruct program budgets using a common taxonomy.

## Client Services and Other Activities

In demonstration projects, staffing costs are further understood by separating the cost of time spent by staff in providing services to clients from the cost of time spent by staff on other activities. Other activities include project development, training, presentations, meetings, and the like. This type of analysis requires the use of time sheets to record the amount of time spent on each type of activity. Each person assigned to the project would fill out a time sheet, regardless of the percentage of time spent on the project. In the analysis of family preservation services, information can be gathered using service logs that capture services provided to the family and/or on time sheets that report worker activities, including client services.

Analysis of work loads is significant for managers who seek to understand both the unit cost of service and the ability of employees to carry a certain number of cases. (Unit costs are discussed in the next section.) Family preservation services caseloads range from 2-3 families per worker to 8-12 families per worker, but, to date, a definitive analysis of worker expended time has not been conducted. We do know that the variation in "down time" among workers may be a result of inconsistent flow of referrals, overly stringent project eligibility criteria, and/or scheduling of staff (Yuan, McDonald, Anderson, & Struckman-Johnson, 1988). Cost analysis can further our understanding of these issues in relation to productivity and cost-effectiveness.

## Public Agency Costs

Data from public agencies that have established intensive in-home services cost centers and that maintain time logs for each worker will be more comparable than data from agencies that have not established such cost centers. However, public agencies may have difficulties in determining costs because of the formulas used for budgeting. The sole means of calculating costs may be to use the salaries of personnel involved. This discounts the costs of buildings, training, supplies, and so on, which are obviously as important to public as to private delivery of service. Ancillary public costs of providing placement prevention services and/or placement services that often are not included in the calculation of actual costs include case management and other services provided by the child welfare public agency, court services, and other services provided by non-child welfare agencies, including schooling, medical services, and counseling services. In one model, the National Resource Center on Family Based Services (1983) used salaries and benefits of public agency staff with an arbitrary multiplier for establishing the indirect cost to determine the cost of the public service. This calculation may incorporate the costs of some of the indirect services, but it is unlikely to cover all ancillary services being provided by the agency.

**Additional Issues**

In reviewing budgets and invoices as data for detailing the cost of service, some other issues are also relevant for the evaluator.

*Stability of program development.* Start-up costs for new programs can be expensive and can detract from the ongoing costs of delivering a service (R. Davidson, personal communication, 1987). If one is trying to determine a cost per client or a cost per service, it becomes important to try to determine whether the period used was one of relative stability or whether it had some major ancillary and/or short-term activities that would affect the cost analysis. For example, if costs are detailed during a period of heavy training of staff, the researcher will need to consider this factor when attempting to determine the ongoing cost of the service. Demonstration programs are prone to changes in staff, heavy investment in establishing community linkages, training of staff, ineffective recruitment, and modifications in the service design; all of these factors may have an impact upon the utilization of time and resources for direct client services.

*Organization variables.* Often, innovative services are provided by either large stable organizations or small new agencies. While these may not differ in outcomes of clients or services delivered, they can have significant differences in direct and indirect costs. The salaries of project staff and administrative staff are often determined by the history and function of the agency, as well as by the program responsibilities. Even agencies with similar salaries may have great variation in other expenditures or allocation of expenditures. For example, one project might use 5% of its $150,000 grant for administrative staff and other nondirect service staff, while another project might use 15% of its grant to cover such costs.

When comparing salaries across projects, the evaluator will need to consider the qualifications for the position, the cost of living in the project area, the fringe benefits calculations of each project, and the standard number of hours allocated to full-time and part-time positions. (Throughout the country, agencies commonly use 35, 37, or 40 hours to represent the full-time workweek.)

*Volunteers and donated materials.* If volunteers are used for specific services, this decreases the cost of service delivery to both the provider and the funder. However, in determining the cost of service, the dollar value of these services and any donated items might be calculated, so as to determine what would need to be paid if all services had to be reimbursed. Minimally, an evaluator should state whether these factors are included in the analysis.

### Summary of Steps for Calculating Program Costs

The following steps are recommended in describing annual program costs:

- Establish the period of analysis, choosing a stable period of operation.

- Determine service staff costs, including full-time, part-time, and consultant staff.
- Determine the other direct costs of service, including other staff and a standard list of allowable direct cost items.
- Determine the indirect costs of service using a standard list of allowable indirect cost items.
- Determine the cost of service for the period by summing the cost of service staff, other direct costs, and indirect costs.
- Add to this cost-of-service calculation the value of volunteered time and donated items, if appropriate.
- Annualize the total project costs over a 12-month period.
- Add to this figure any additional one-time expenditures.

## *Establishing Service Unit Costs*

The importance of variations in methods of attributing costs can be somewhat minimized if a unit cost analysis is undertaken. In order to compare costs of different projects, the evaluator needs to establish a cost for each unit of service, whether the unit of service is based on a number of clients, type of service, or length of time. In this section, several ways of calculating unit costs are discussed.

### Client Unit Costs

One type of unit cost is the per client cost. A per client cost is determined by dividing the total program cost, or some portion of the total program cost, by the number of clients served. However, evaluators of family preservation services programs are faced with a dilemma that is also faced by other evaluators of human services programs. Who is the client? Is the client the family, or the children in the family, or the child or children at risk of placement?

For family preservation services programs, it is recommended that evaluators consider both the per family cost and the per child cost. To date, some family preservation services have calculated costs per family and others per child. This has resulted in consid-

**Table 6.2** Costs per Family and per Child

|  |  | Model A $ | Model B $ |
|---|---|---|---|
| Cost per family |  | 5,000 |  |
| Per child cost if: | 1 child | 5,000 |  |
|  | 2 children | 2,500 |  |
|  | 3 children | 1,667 |  |
|  | 4 children | 1,250 |  |
| Cost per child |  |  | 2,000 |
| Per family cost if: | 1 child |  | 2,000 |
|  | 2 children |  | 4,000 |
|  | 3 children |  | 6,000 |
|  | 4 children |  | 8,000 |

erable confusion in the literature, with costs per child sometimes being reported as costs per family. Given that family preservation programs provide services to a family unit, and most of them determine that the family is the client from the therapeutic point of view, it is sensible to consider the family unit when determining costs. However, one of the comparisons of most interest to readers of evaluation reports is the savings accrued from preventing placement. This analysis requires consideration on the per child cost. More specifically, if the referral source can identify the number of children at risk of placement in the family, the per child cost may utilize the number of children determined to be at risk.

If the cost is calculated per child, or per child at risk of placement, the per client cost will decrease as the number of children served increases. For example, let us hypothesize that a project spent $150,000 on serving 40 families. The per family cost of service in this case would be $3,750. If there were 75 children in these 40 families, the per child cost would be $2,000. If there were 95 children in these 40 families, the per child cost would be $1,578.95. If there were only 40 children identified as at risk of placement, the cost per child at risk of placement would be $3,750.

As shown in Table 6.2, the implication of two alternative methods of determining costs can affect future allocations of resources for programs. If costs are calculated primarily on a family basis, the cost per child decreases within each family as the number of children increases. The result is similar to the procedure used by day-care centers that offer discounts for caring for multiple children in a family (Elliot & Forman, 1980). If the costs are calculated on a per child basis, the cost for each child remains the same, but the cost per family increases with the number of children in the family. For example, if an agency is paid $2,000 per child, a family of one child would be served at a cost of $2,000, a family of two children at a cost of $4,000, and a family of three children at $6,000.

## Hourly Unit Costs

Definitions of costs per family or per child that do not examine the amount of service delivered assume that all families are receiving similar amounts of service. For example, a counseling program that provides 20 hours of counseling per family could establish a family cost recognizing that all families receive 20 hours of service. The client cost would be readily comparable to an hourly cost. In a family preservation program, if there is variability in amount of service provided per family there can be significant impact upon costs, work load, and service efficiency.

For example, if an agency spends $4,000 per month and serves three families during that month, the per family cost is $1,333. On the other hand, if this $4,000 reflects the utilization of 240 hours, each hour is worth $16.67, and the actual cost per client would vary with the actual number of hours of service provided. One client may have utilized half of the service hours, while each of the other two clients used only a quarter of the hours.

**Table 6.3** Service Hours Provided to Families by Two Projects

|  | Project A | | | | | | Project B | | | | | |
|  | Family 1 | 2 | 3 | 4 | 5 | Total Hours | Family 6 | 7 | 8 | 9 | 10 | Total Hours |
|---|---|---|---|---|---|---|---|---|---|---|---|---|
| Number of hours per family |  | 55 | 49 | 38 | 33 | 42 | 217 | | 35 | 27 | 36 | 25 | 32 | 155 |

In family preservation services, the per hour cost is an important one, because it can be useful in explaining the range of cases handled by programs. Some programs serve fewer families per worker over a shorter period of time, while others serve more families per worker over a longer period of time. If the per hour cost is similar, then the services can be determined to be comparable and length of service or intensity of service or some other variable may be analyzed.

Let us compare two hypothetical programs with regard to cost per hour. Both programs served five families over a period of two months at a cost of $18,750. The per family cost for each program is the same: $3,750. Further examination of the data shows that there were no significant differences in either the number of children in the families or the number of adults in the families. However, when the number of direct and collateral hours of services per family is analyzed, differences in unit cost are revealed.

As seen in Table 6.3, the average number of hours per family is 43.4; in Project B, the average number of hours per family is 31. In Project A, the cost per hour of service is $86.41. In Project B, the cost per hour of service is $120.97, a 40% difference in cost. If we hypothesize that in each project there are 240 hours of staff time available, Project A is using 90% of its time in service hours and Project B is using 65% of its time in service hours. Thus the method of calculating costs will not only affect the end unit cost, but can also shed significant light on the program's approach to providing services.

## Service Unit Costs

Measuring unit costs by number of hours of service does not address the types of services that are being provided. Defining expenditure of time in terms of types of services is extremely problematic for family preservation programs, which often provide many services using one worker or therapist. In working with families, workers may be able to delineate which services they are providing, but since the same worker may provide several services during one "session," the evaluator may have access only to aggregate service information.

Examining types of services in greater detail can, however, illuminate the issue of cost from another perspective. The amount of time used to provide specific service activities, such as counseling, parent training, legal assistance, and so on, could be calculated for each family and then the distribution of services across clients or programs compared. An example of such an analysis is provided below.

For example, let us hypothesize that Project C expends an average of 45 hours per family and that 65% of that time is spent in counseling services; 25% is spent in transporting the family, locating housing, and arranging other services; and 10% is used in indirect client services such as record keeping and preparing for court. Project D expends an average of 45 hours per family and 50% of the time is spent in transporting the family, locating housing, chore assistance, and so on; 40% in counseling; and 10% in record keeping. Since one worker is providing all services, the cost per service unit does not vary except as a function of time. However, the evaluation might result in recommendations concerning staffing patterns that could reduce costs and increase the efficiency of the program. While not strictly cost analysis, such examinations of time and service data can provide management with useful service philosophy and service cost information.

In order to conduct such an analysis, workers will need to keep accurate and detailed records of the use of their time, and resources will need to be provided for analyzing the data. With limited resources, such a detailed study might be conducted for only a subset of the family cases.

## Other Measures of Unit Costs

Zelman (1987) discusses several alternative means of calculating unit costs when family services are delivered by a team. Zelman computes units of service based on taking into consideration elapsed time, number of service personnel, and number of recipients. When one hour of service is provided to these family members by two psychologists, the unit of service can range from one hour, if elapsed time is counted, to six hours, if face-to-face time is calculated for each participant. If the evaluator is interested in staff time and a team of workers is used, then the attribution of one hour to both workers explains the utilization of staff time. If the evaluator is interested in client time and assumes that each member of the family is a client, then each member has spent one hour with two therapists and, in terms of service, each member has received two hours of staff time.

Maximization of unit costs is an issue that the evaluator may need to address. If one worker sees 20 families a year at a cost of $56,000, the cost per family is $2,800. If another worker sees 24 families in a year at a cost of $56,000, the per family cost is $2,333. However, if the first worker averages 60 hours per family, at a cost of $46.67 per hour, and the second worker averages 40 hours per family at a cost of $58.33, the second worker is more expensive in terms of hours of service provided than the first worker.

The analysis may be further complicated by the use of teams in one case and single therapists in another. Let us hypothesize that the first worker uses a paraprofessional in a teaming arrangement. One could calculate that each family has received 120 hours of service and that therefore the per hour cost is $23.33.

The options provided by Zelman (1987) also introduce the interesting concept of the cost to the family in receiving the service. Although few if any family preservation services are being provided through fee-for-service arrangements, the investment by the family, in terms of time, is nevertheless significant. Indeed, the cost of the service to the adult members of the family is greater in terms of time expended by the family than if other services such as individual counseling or substitute care were provided. Family preservation services presume that families consider substitute care a negative condition and therefore will participate in intensive in-home service in order to avoid the placement of their children. However, if a family sees placement as providing positive services, then that family might weigh the costs of both alternatives in choosing which service to accept. Future cost-benefit studies will need to investigate the value structure of the participants in the service as well as the monetary and nonmonetary costs to them (see Wald, 1988).

### Unit Cost Recommendations

The following types of unit cost analysis can be useful in understanding family preservation services programs:

- *cost per family:* program costs divided by the number of families served
- *cost per child at risk of placement:* program costs divided by the number of children identified as at risk of placement
- *cost per hour of service:* program costs divided by the number of direct and collateral hours of service
- *cost per service type:* types of services analyzed and percentage of time used for each service type calculated; total program costs multiplied by these percentages

## Comparing Family Preservation Services to Alternative Services

The most common comparison used in cost analysis of family preservation services is between the in-home program and substitute care. This section discusses the methodology used to establish this comparison and other family outcome comparisons.

## Comparisons with Substitute Care

The current practice in calculating the costs of substitute care is to utilize established rate structures and then to project savings over time. Age-specific substitute care rates, in addition to other maintenance fees, are taken into consideration when determining the cost of alternative services such as placement. For state and local governments these are the first line of attack when considering cost savings, since they represent easily identifiable significant expenditures by the agency.

However, these costs are only part of the cost of substitute care. Rates for substitute care may differ from the actual costs of care. There are additional costs that may be difficult to quantify, such as the cost to the public agency of developing, licensing, monitoring, and regulating these resources. Also unknown may be the expenses of such care borne by providers and other recognized system participants, such as the courts. Unless there is a separate process of developing a comprehensive picture of children's services costs, the evaluator may be limited to working with the available data and using approximate costs for analysis.

Chapter 5 of this volume discusses various measures of placement after receiving services, and this topic is not expanded upon here. It is important to recognize, however, that a cost analysis of savings incurred by family preservation services is probably as limited by the ability to collect follow-up data, including placement by different agencies, as by cost analysis methodologies (Michigan Department of Social Services, 1983).

There are three alternative approaches to determining the length of time in substitute care that can be used in making comparisons of cost. One alternative is to consider the average length of time in substitute care and to project savings by calculating the cost of this average length of time in care. This method of projection has not been validated due to the lack of follow-up data on families for extended periods of time. Another alternative is to conduct follow-up studies on the children served by family preservation services and to calculate savings based on the known period of time that each child has remained at home and has not been placed (AuClaire & Schwartz, 1986). This method is grounded in actual client data, and is a more conservative approach than using projected lengths of stay. The disadvantage to using this approach is that the evaluation study must continue over a longer period of time in order to follow up on families.

A third alternative is to compare a group that receives family preservation services with a group that does not receive such services. This approach compares the "success rates" of both the served group and the control group and then determines the savings for each group in order to establish a more accurate picture of the cost savings resulting from family preservation services. Such an evaluation study may require additional resources in order to develop a control group and to follow both the control and treatment groups.

Let us hypothesize that 80% of 100 children served in a family preservation services program remained out of placement for 12 months, while 20% were placed for 8 months of the year. If the cost of placement is $250 per month per child, the placement expenditures decreased from $300,000 to $40,000. However, if the cost of serving these 100 children in family preservation services was $2,000 per child, $200,000 has been expended, and there are net savings of $60,000.

If all of the children in the control group are placed, then one may assume that the family preservation services program has produced the savings. If, however, a number of children are not placed, then the analysis will need to consider cost savings that can be attributed to the traditional services received by the control group.

Let us hypothesize that of the 100 children in the control group, 90 were placed for 12 months and 10 remained at home for 12 months. Placement costs were therefore $270,000 rather than

$300,000. If one uses $270,000 as the comparison figure, then the family preservation program has saved $30,000 rather than $60,000.

Although the accuracy of projected savings has not yet been tested, such projections may be useful for planning purposes. Projected savings are influenced by the method of calculating intensive in-home costs. If the cost of service is calculated on a per family basis, the fewer children in the family, the longer the projected period of substitute care, or the more costly the type of care must be in order to achieve significant savings. For example, if family preservation services cost $2,800 per family and the foster care rate is $243 per child per month, a savings of more than $3,000 will accrue if two children are projected to be placed for 12 months in foster care or four children are projected to be placed for 6 months in foster care. Savings increase dramatically with the number of children at risk of placement and the length of time it is projected that they would be in care.

On the other hand, if family preservation services are paid on a per child basis, and the cost per child is $1,700 and foster care rates are $243 per child per month, the cost of providing family preservation services increases per child, but savings per child remain the same.

The data provided in Tables 6.4 and 6.5 exemplify the use of cost data in resource utilization planning. Such data can also be used for determining standards of performance, if an amount of savings is targeted.

In the above examples, we use foster care rates for calculating costs of placement. Children are, however, placed in different types of resources, and the costs of these resources vary greatly. Care should be taken in projecting savings. Since placement decisions are based upon availability as well as need, projections using the most costly type of care can result in inflated cost savings. Increased attention to utilization of foster care resources by the local community could perhaps generate predictive models based upon client

**Table 6.4**  Savings in Avoiding 6 Months or 12 Months of Foster Care: Model A

*Premises:    Family preservation services cost per family is $2,800.*
*Foster care rate is $243 per child per month.*

| Number of Children and per Child FPS Cost | | 6 Months of Foster Care per Family ($) | 12 Months of Foster Care per Family ($) | 6 Months' Savings per Family ($) | 12 Months' Savings per Family ($) |
|---|---|---|---|---|---|
| 1 | 2,800 | 1,458 | 2,916 | none | 116 |
| 2 | 1,400 | 2,916 | 5,832 | 116 | 3,032 |
| 3 | 933 | 4,374 | 8,748 | 1,574 | 5,948 |
| 4 | 700 | 5,832 | 11,664 | 3,032 | 8,864 |
| Savings per child: | 1 child in the family | | | none | 116.00 |
| | 2 children in the family | | | 58.00 | 1,516.00 |
| | 3 children in the family | | | 524.67 | 1,982.67 |
| | 4 children in the family | | | 758.00 | 2,216.00 |

Findings:

The fewer children in the family, the longer the length of projected length of care must be for comparable savings. For example, to save $3,032, 2 children need to be in care for 12 months or 4 children for 6 months.

If family preservation services are paid for on a per family basis, the savings increase dramatically with the number of children in substitute care and the length of placement.

In this hypothetical example, the length of time of follow-up should be one year in order to monitor significant savings.

characteristics, resource availability, and worker judgments, which then could further refine the calculations of cost savings.

The prior discussion hypothesizes that the children will be placed in the same types of placement for the same amount of time. There is evidence that this may not occur. AuClaire and Schwartz (1986) demonstrate that children who received intensive services and were placed stayed shorter periods of time and in less intensive resources. Nevertheless, the example provided here is simplified in order to illustrate the point that cost savings are definitely linked to the cost of service.

**Table 6.5** Savings in Avoiding 6 Months or 12 Months of Foster Care: Model B

*Premises:    Family preservation services cost per child is $1,700.*
*Foster care rate is $243 per child per month.*

| Number of Children and FPS Cost per Family ($) | 6 Months of Foster Care per Family ($) | 12 Months of Foster Care per Family ($) | 6 Months' Savings per Family ($) | 12 Months' Savings per Family ($) |
|---|---|---|---|---|
| 1    1,700 | 1,458 | 2,916 | none | 1,216 |
| 2    3,400 | 2,916 | 5,832 | none | 2,432 |
| 3    5,100 | 4,374 | 8,748 | none | 3,468 |
| 4    6,800 | 5,832 | 11,664 | none | 4,864 |
| Savings per child: | 1 child in the family | | | 1,216 |
| | 2 children in the family | | | 1,216 |
| | 3 children in the family | | | 1,216 |
| | 4 children in the family | | | 1,216 |

Findings:

If payments are per child it takes a greater number of days in care to result in savings.

The cost per family increases per child, but the savings per child remain the same.

The higher the cost of foster care, the greater the increment in cost savings over time regardless of cost of providing in-home services.

The longer the predicted length in care, the greater the cost savings.

## Additional Cost Impact Issues

Since the potential savings from preventing placement are so great, there has been little calculation of other service costs that the family may incur subsequent to receiving family preservation services. At a resource planning level, this information might be of great significance, since there may be increased demand upon other family-based services as a result of family preservation services. Increased demands on day care, respite care, and educational services are easily envisioned. The impact of family preservation services may be to decrease one class of expenditures while increasing another class of expenditures.

**Comparisons with Other Prevention Services**

To date, there have been only a few studies that have compared the costs of alternative prevention programs. The comprehensive review of child abuse and neglect demonstration projects (U.S. Department of Health, Education and Welfare, 1978) developed detailed estimates of the costs of different service models for eleven projects. The National Clinical Evaluation Study of 19 demonstration projects also collected detailed cost data (see Daro, 1988). There have also been attempts to compare the costs of other protective service caseloads with caseloads of family-based services. Further research is needed to examine family preservation services and alternative service strategies in the same community and to detail the costs of each service with regard to outcomes.

As the understanding of both service inputs and service outputs grows, it is conceivable that further studies will be able to compare the costs of providing different types of family-based service models with their resultant outcomes and to apply outcome measures related to family stability, reduction of violence, and so on to cost analysis. Such studies will be able to determine with a greater degree of accuracy which options are most cost-effective for an agency (Sorensen & Binner, 1979).

Cost analyses may indicate that there are equal savings to be achieved from less expensive programs. For example, traditional protective services may have lower rates of preventing placement and yet still result in savings. Let us hypothesize that 100 children are served at a cost of $800 per child in a placement prevention program. If we consider that the cost of substitute care is $250 per month per child and that 12 months of placement for 100 children will cost $300,000, in order to save $40,000 the placement prevention program has to have a success rate of 40%. Since 60 children placed for one year will cost $180,000 and to serve 100 children will cost $80,000, the cost of the service plus the cost of placement will total $260,000, with a net savings of $40,000.

This example points out the problem of developing cost-benefit analyses for such programs. Although other services may result in equal savings with less expenditure, it may be that there are certain outcomes that are not achieved, or that there are additional costs of the family preservation services program that make the comparison even more dramatic. The ability to conduct cost-benefit analyses is dependent upon the ability to conduct adequate outcome analyses. The intrinsic complexities of conducting cost analyses coupled with the difficulties of establishing and measuring outcomes of families should lead evaluators and policy analysts to use caution in their discussions of cost-benefits. Certainly much work remains to be done in our effort to understand the comparison of the costs and impacts of family preservation services with the costs and impacts of alternative services.

## *Conclusion*

In analyzing the cost of service, an evaluator can fulfill several roles. The first is to complement the role of the accountant by relating the cost of service to the parameters of service and establishing a baseline cost of service. The second is to elucidate the unit cost of service so as to establish a means of comparing different family preservation programs. In conducting this work, the evaluator can provide useful information to program administrators and planners who are implementing the service past the demonstration phase. The third is a role that may require special study and, as such, may be beyond the scope of work of many evaluators. This entails an analysis of the cost savings and cost-benefits of family preservation services.

In order to operationalize cost analysis, the following suggestions are made to evaluators:

(1) Use a stable period of time in conducting the analysis.
(2) Establish the total program cost for that period, excluding any unusual expenses that may skew the analysis.
(3) Calculate the per family cost and the per child cost by dividing the total program cost by the relevant client unit.

(4) Calculate the per hour service cost by dividing the program costs by the hours of service provided.

(5) Establish the ratio of service hours to administrative hours or nonclient service hours and establish the percentage of program costs used for services and other activities.

(6) If resources and data are available, compare the types of service activities and establish the cost per type of service.

(7) Use the above analysis to assist program administrators in determining the efficiency of resource utilization.

(8) Calculate cost savings by utilizing the most conservative comparison, namely, actual length of time out of placement multiplied by least expensive cost of placement, unless other data are available.

(9) If the outcome data are available and resources are sufficient, undertake to establish the cost-benefits of family preservation services.

Program administrators who are interested in gaining a greater understanding of the costs of developing and implementing such programs, and who plan to use a project evaluator to assist them in the analysis, should seek consultation during the design of the fiscal reporting procedures in order to facilitate the cost analysis evaluation activities.

Many evaluators will not be able to undertake the full scope of cost-related evaluation studies. Indeed, special studies may be needed to assess the cost-benefits of such programs accurately (Ciarlo & Windle, 1988). Policymakers will need to decide the extent to which accurate information is required for future planning and support studies that can address their specific programmatic and/or cross-program planning.

## References

The selected references listed here do not represent the entire field on cost analysis issues. In 1979, Project SHARE published a bibliography titled *Approaches to Budgeting and Cost Analysis,* but this is now out of date and out of print. The references listed below represent some of the more recent works that have provided helpful data for this chapter.

AuClaire, P., & Schwartz, I. (1986). *An evaluation of the effectiveness of intensive home-based services as an alternative to placement for adolescents and their families*. Minneapolis: Hennepin County Community Services Department and University of Minnesota, Hubert H. Humphrey Institute of Public Affairs.

Ciarlo, J. A., & Windle, C. (1988). Mental health program evaluation and needs assessment. In H. S. Bloom, D. S. Cordray, & R. L. Light (Eds.), Lessons from selected program and policy areas [Special issue]. *New Directions for Program Evaluation, 37*, 99-120.

Collins, R. C. (1987). *Foster care rates: Trends and implications* (Child Welfare Research Note 17). Washington, DC: U.S. Department of Health and Human Services.

Copeland, W. C., & Iversen, I. A. (1981). *Refinancing and reorganizing human services: Interagency net budgeting and other fiscal incentives* (Project SHARE Human Services Monograph Series 20). Washington, DC: U.S. Department of Health and Human Services.

Daro, D. (1988). *Confronting child abuse*. New York: Free Press.

Elliot, P., & Forman, J. (1980). *Analyzing costs in human service programs, procedures manual* (Vol. 2). Washington, DC: U.S. Department of Health and Human Services.

Hagedorn, H. J., Beck, K., Neubert, S., & Werlin, S. H. (1976). *A working manual of simple program evaluation techniques for community mental health centers*. Rockville, MD: National Institute of Mental Health.

Kinney, J., Godfrey, C., Haapala, D., & Madsen, B. (1979). Homebuilders: Keeping families together. In G. Landsberg, W. D. Neigher, R. J. Hammer, C. Windle, & J. R. Woy (Eds.), *Evaluation in practice: A sourcebook of program evaluation studies from mental health care systems in the United States* (DHHS Publication No. ADM 80-763) (pp. 196-197). Washington, DC: Government Printing Office.

Koshel, J., & Kinney, J. (1986). *Family preservation: The Homebuilders' Program in the State of Washington*. Washington, DC: National Governors' Association.

Michigan Department of Social Services, Office of Children and Youth Services. (1983). *A study of direct and purchased foster care placement services in Michigan*. Lansing: Author.

National Resource Center on Family Based Services. (1983). *Family centered social services: A model for child welfare agencies*. Oakdale, IA: Author.

Richardson, D. A. (1981). *Rate setting in the human services: A guide for administrators* (Project SHARE, Human Services Monograph Series). Washington DC: U.S. Department of Health and Human Services.

Robison, S. (1987). *State child welfare reform: Toward a family based policy*. Denver: National Conference of State Legislatures.

Smith, N. L., & Smith, J. K. (1985). State level evaluation uses of cost analysis: A national descriptive study. In J. S. Catterall (Ed.), Economic evaluation of public programs [Special issue]. *New Directions for Program Evaluation, 26*, 83-96.

Smith, S. (1986). *Child welfare in the states: Fifty state survey report*. Denver: National Conference of State Legislatures.

Sorensen, J., & Binner, P. (1979). Overview of cost, cost outcome, cost effectiveness. In G. Landsberg, W. D. Neigher, R. J. Hammer, C. Windle, & J. R. Woy (Eds.), *Evaluation in practice: A sourcebook of program evaluation studies from mental health care systems in the United States* (DHHS Publication No. ADM 80-763) (pp. 183-189). Washington, DC: Government Printing Office.

U.S. Department of Health and Human Services, Office of Human Development Services, Grants and Contracts Management Division/OMS. (1986). *Discretionary grants administration manual.* Washington, DC: Author.

U.S. Department of Health, Education and Welfare. (1978). *Evaluation of child abuse and neglect demonstration projects, 1974-1977* (Vols. 1, 2, 7) (National Center for Health Services Research Report Series). Washington, DC: Author.

Wald, M. (1988). Family preservation: Are we moving too fast? *Public Welfare, 46*(3), 33-38.

Yuan, Y. Y., McDonald, W. R., Anderson, J., & Struckman-Johnson, D. (1988). *Evaluation of AB 1562 demonstration projects: Year two interim report.* Sacramento, CA: Walter R. McDonald & Associates, Inc.

Zelman, W. (1987). Cost per unit of service. *Evaluation and Program Planning, 10*(3), 201-208.

7

# Study Design

## LEONARD BICKMAN

Family preservation programs, like other social programs, are under pressure to demonstrate their effectiveness. They need to present evidence that they affect families and children in a positive manner. The previous chapters delineated the structure and content of these programs and the types of outcomes that should be their goals. In order to provide unambiguous evidence of effectiveness, the evaluation must be placed in a design framework. This chapter provides design and statistical guidelines. In particular, it focuses on correcting two major design weaknesses. Suggestions are provided on how to increase the ability of the evaluation to detect meaningful program effects and how to attribute these effects to the operation of the program.

Evaluation can serve many functions, including needs assessment, determination of characteristics of clients served, and quality assurance or monitoring. But the ultimate purpose of most evaluations is to determine whether or not the intervention had positive effects on clients. This determination of effectiveness is the bottom line for evaluation. Evidence should be provided that shows that family preservation programs make a positive difference in the lives of children and their families.

This chapter takes a quantitative perspective on outcome evaluations. There are qualitative approaches that can also be used to evaluate projects (see, e.g., Guba, 1987). Qualitative approaches use such techniques as participant observation and are considered credible under some circumstances. They are especially useful when a detailed description of a project is needed and in cases where quantitative evaluation cannot be conducted. However, for outcome evaluations a quantitative approach is preferred.

All evaluations collect data about clients. These data may include frequency of out-of-home placements, academic achievement, or self-esteem of the child. But the data themselves do not indicate whether or not the program is effective. Just knowing that 30% of the children stayed with their families after being in a home-based program does not tell us if the program was effective. An evaluation design requiring comparisons is needed to determine whether or not this outcome can be judged successful. In some designs client data collected before the start of the program are compared to data on the same clients after the program is completed. However, as will be pointed out later, such comparisons are often difficult to interpret. Moreover, for outcome data such as placement, pre-post comparison is not appropriate. To determine whether a program had an effect or not, individuals who received the treatment (experimental group) need to be compared to those who did not receive the treatment (control group). However, it is important that these groups differ only in whether or not they received the treatment. If the groups differ on other factors, then it could be argued that these factors, and not the treatment, contributed to the observed difference. In evaluation terminology these other factors are called *threats to validity.*

This chapter approaches the planning of family preservation outcome evaluations by examining threats to the validity of such evaluations and suggesting ways to deal with those threats. Validity has been discussed extensively by Campbell and his colleagues (Campbell & Stanley, 1966; Cook & Campbell, 1979) as the foundation of research design. In Campbell's scheme there are four types of validity: statistical conclusion validity, internal validity, construct validity, and external validity.

The evaluation must be designed so that it will uncover an important outcome if one really exists (statistical validity), be able to credit this effect to the program and not to some irrelevant cause (internal validity), identify the proper elements of the program that produced the effect on relevant outcome measures (construct validity), and be able to extend the results to situations other than the one studied (external validity). These four validities can be restated as four questions:

- Are the results statistically significant?
- Did the program cause the effects?
- Can we clearly identify the important aspects of the program that had effects on important and meaningful outcomes?
- Can the results be generalized to other sites, clients, and times?

This chapter focuses on the first two questions, for two reasons. First, other chapters in this volume cover construct validity. Previous chapters have discussed the content of family preservation programs and the selection of instruments that should measure the outcomes of family preservation programs. External validity is an important concern for multisite evaluations but not of high priority for planning individual local program evaluations. Second, statistical conclusion validity and internal validity usually pose more difficult planning obstacles and typically cause more problems for evaluators than the other two validities. However, both construct and external validity are briefly described in the following subsections.

**Construct Validity**

Construct validity is concerned with both the measures of program outcome and the nature of the program. In the former case the question is whether the outcome measures are valid representations of the constructs thought to underlie those measures. This is a conceptual question that attempts to relate the measures or outcomes of the evaluation to what these outcomes are supposed to measure. For example, we could possibly measure running away behavior by asking the child if he or she had ever run away, or we might use law enforcement records. Each of these measures has problems with construct validity. The child's report might be distorted because of intentional lying, because of forgetting, or because the child's definition of running away might be different from the investigator's. Official records may also present a distorted view of running away behaviors. Incidents might not have been reported, the police might not have recorded reports accurately, or files might have been lost. All of these are threats to the construct validity of the particular operationalization of the concept of running away behavior. Cook and Campbell (1979) describe a number of threats to construct validity, including evaluation apprehension, confounding, single method bias, and measure biases.

Construct validity refers not only to the outcome measures but also to the cause of the effect, namely, the program. Causal construct validity is important if we are to understand properly which features of the program are responsible for a significant effect. What are the key elements of the program that are necessary to produce the desired outcome? Is it the shortness of time between referral and first contact? Is it the low caseload of the project worker? Is it the particular social work theory followed by the counselors, or the motivation and management of the program staff? All of these factors need to be considered in describing the program; collectively, they have been referred to as the "program theory" (Bickman, 1987). The theory underlying the program needs to be explicated if we are going to be able to replicate the key aspects of the program. Suggestions for improving construct validity can be found in the chapters dealing with measurement and program description.

## External Validity

The term *external validity* refers to the generalizability of the findings of the evaluation to other settings, clients, and times. A policymaker needs to know if a program that was demonstrated to be successful in a particular evaluation could be successfully replicated in a different location with somewhat different clients and at a different time in history. Threats to external validity include interaction of selection and treatment, of setting and treatment, and of history and treatment (Cook & Campbell, 1979). External validity is a significant concern for transferring specific program models.

## A Caution

The guidelines discussed in this chapter are based on high standards for the conduct of outcome evaluations. The criteria include the use of randomized experiments to reduce threats to internal validity and the consideration of statistical power. These may be unrealistically high standards for many family preservation programs, which tend to be small and without extensive resources for evaluation. Because of the difficulty in implementing the suggestions provided in this chapter, quantitative outcome evaluations should not be attempted without sufficient resources, motivation, and ability to conduct technically correct evaluations. Poorly implemented evaluations are a disservice to the field and to programs. Outcome evaluations should be undertaken only when successful implementation of the evaluation design is likely. This chapter provides suggestions to help the planner decide whether or not that is probable.

## *The Internal Validity of the Design*

### What Is Internal Validity?

Given that the results of the evaluation are statistically significant, the next question to consider is whether they are due to the program. Did the program cause the effects? The primary purpose of the evaluation design is to demonstrate that the program, and only the program, produced the effects discovered. There are a number of threats to internal validity to consider in designing a family preservation evaluation. These threats are plausible alternatives to the conclusion that the family preservation program caused a positive outcome, such as reduction in running away behavior among children. These threats masquerade as program effects and are often confused with them unless the evaluation is designed to reduce their plausibility. Using running away behavior as an example, a brief review of four threats that are particularly relevant to family preservation programs is offered below. Cook and Campbell (1979) provide an extensive review of threats to internal validity.

(1) *Maturation.* It is possible that adolescents run away less frequently as they get older. Thus without any intervention we would expect that 18-year-olds will run away less frequently than 16-year-olds. If an evaluation simply compares a group of children at age 16 when they entered the program with the same children at age 18, the program may be labeled successful when in fact maturation accounted for the change.

(2) *Selection.* All evaluations require a comparison. In the above example the children's running away behavior was compared at ages 16 and 18. In most evaluations a group of untreated families will be used as the comparison or control group. One of the major problems in conducting family preservation evaluations is the selection of the comparisons. Ideally, the comparison group should be exactly like the treatment group in all ways except for the treatment. The more differences that exist initially between these two groups, the higher the probability that these differences could explain any results found. For example, if we compare running away frequency of two groups two years after the program, we might conclude that the program was successful if the treatment group had fewer instances of running away. However, an alternative explanation is that the children selected into the program had fewer of those behaviors at the start of the program. Unless we knew that the children were alike before the start of the program, we could not be sure that any differences found after the program was completed were due to the program and not to initial differences.

(3) *History.* Often something will occur between the initiation and completion of a program that could affect an outcome variable that is not related to any of the program activities. These other factors, known collectively as history, are changes in the environment that could be confused with program effects. In family preservation programs this could be the existence of other programs. For example, if the schools also instituted a program that dealt with youth who had problems in school, this could also affect running away behavior. This problem is especially acute when the treatment group children are exposed to other programs but the comparison group children are not. Evaluators need to keep track of other programs that could affect their evaluation.

(4) *Regression artifacts.* A more subtle threat to internal validity is regression to the mean. This is especially true of programs that are designed to treat individuals who have problems. In most programs, if there is a larger number of clients than the program can treat, individuals believed to have the most severe problems are given priority because they are seen as having the greatest need. If these individuals are compared after the program is completed with those not selected, it is possible that a seemingly positive outcome was due to regression. This may not appear to make much sense given that the program chose the apparently more difficult cases; it would seem that these families would be the most difficult cases to treat. However, this assumes that the initial measurement of the number of problems was validly assessed. If there is some unreliability in this measurement (and there almost always is), then this unreliability can make it seem that there was an effect when there was not. This result is obtained because the families selected for treatment had the most problems *at one point in time*. Since the number of problems a family has at any point in time is due in part to chance, the next time they are measured it is probable that the number of problems will regress to the group grand mean, which will naturally be lower than the initial number of problems for the treatment group. This regression artifact is most likely to occur when a treatment group is selected for their extreme scores and when there is unreliability of measurement. This threat is lessened when it can be shown that the number of problems is a very stable indicator.

Other threats described by Cook and Campbell (1979) include testing, instrumentation, mortality, and selection interactions. The reader is referred to that volume for further explanation.

**Methods for Improving Internal Validity**

*Random Assignment*

Random assignment is the method that best controls for threats to internal validity and is most efficient in its estimates of true treatment effects. Competently implemented, random assignment assures that the persons in the treatment group are equivalent to those in the control group. No other design can assure this as well as the randomized experiment. Randomized experiments also produce statistical estimates that are more easily interpreted. However, compared with other methods, they are often difficult to implement. Legal objections are sometimes raised when the use of randomized experiments is suggested, but Boruch and Wothke (1985) point out that when the use of random assignment has been challenged in the courts it has been ruled as legal. Second, in answer to arguments concerning the feasibility of randomized experiments, Boruch compiled a list of more than 300 successful randomized field tests ten years ago (Boruch, McSweeny, & Soderstrom, 1978). There are a number of practical suggestions for the implementation of randomized field experiments.

(1) *Planning for failure.* As previously demonstrated by Boruch, randomized experiments are feasible. Even under adverse and unstable conditions, these designs usually hold together. However, if a randomized experiment is planned, the evaluator also needs to develop fallback strategies in case he or she is not able to implement the design. These include the use of quasi-experiments, which will be described later in this chapter.

(2) *Obtaining and assigning clients.*

    (a) *Determine eligibility for the program before assignment.* If this is not done it is likely that there will be differential attribution after random assignment. This will invalidate the design.

(b) *Use an unbiased method of random assignment.* Random assignment is not the same as haphazard assignment. The procedures used should ensure that all eligible clients have an equal chance of being assigned to the treatment or control group.

(c) *Stratify to reduce variance.* A process that can be used to reduce variance is stratifying before random assignment. Stratification has been used with pretest data, such as reading scores, and unit size, such as school size. In each case, units were first matched and then randomly assigned. This can be applied to family preservation programs by matching on SES or severity of problems.

(d) *Use alternative services.* In family preservation services a waiting list is usually considered inappropriate with program design because client flow is not high enough. An alternative service may be offered by the program. The comparison will then be between the experimental treatment and some alternative treatment. If there are sufficient resources to treat all potential clients it will be much more difficult to convince the program staff that some clients should not receive the program treatment. Ethical issues are usually raised at this point. It may be considered unethical to deny treatment to families that are in need. The counterargument to this position is that it may not be ethical to treat individuals with a specific program that has not yet demonstrated its effectiveness. The purpose of the evaluation is to establish the program's efficacy. It is premature to assume that it is effective or more effective than other programs. It could also be argued that the long-range gain to these clients and future clients is in establishing, with as much certainty as possible, that the treatment is efficacious. Finally, in almost all cases the family preservation program is not the sole source of service to these clients. The existing social service system is the actual "no treatment" comparison group for family preservation projects.

(e) *Use randomization with a sample of clients.* If the program personnel insist that clients with the most severe problems receive services first, then it may be argued that clients at the lower end of the severity scale, for which it is not clear whether they should receive priority, be randomly assigned to treatment and control conditions. That is, use random assignment for clients deemed to be of lower priority. However, this will result in a randomized experiment for a smaller number of clients whose range of severity is reduced. This will weaken the generalizability of the evaluation.

(3) *Reduce attrition.* The major problem faced in many randomized studies is attrition. It is recommended that, in a field setting, the evaluator take the following steps:

(a) *Delay the random assignment as long as possible,* preferably after the pretest data have been collected.

(b) *Obtain prior agreement from volunteers to be in either the control or the treatment group.* Inform volunteers that if they agree to participate in the program they have a probability of being assigned to a treatment or control group. Do not include those potential clients in the study who do not agree to this basic stipulation. This approach provides full disclosure about the nature of the evaluation and should satisfy an institutional review board's concern with the treatment of human subjects.

(c) *Use incentives.* If it is necessary to contact the control group, incentives (such as payment) to keep that group intact to reduce differential attrition should be considered.

(d) *Verify client flow and availability.* Obtain nonoptimistic and accurate estimates of the yield of volunteers if statistical power is going to be maintained. The evaluator must have confidence in (and must verify) estimates of voluntary participation. Shortfalls in this area will mean recruiting more units, after random assignment, at a possible cost to the integrity of the design. The level of referrals needs to be high enough to sustain both treatment and control groups. The referral agencies should be understanding and supportive of conducting an evaluation that uses random assignment. Without understanding and support, these agencies may be reluctant to make referrals.

Following the above point, if some nested or aggregated design is being used, assurances from or control of the unit that is randomly assigned does not assure that the individuals in that unit will participate. Thus referring agencies' assurance of cooperation does not guarantee that their clients will participate. The evaluator needs to be sensitive to site and individual attrition.

(4) *Use the proper unit of analysis.* To conduct a good randomized experiment, the evaluator should be sensitive to the proper unit of analysis. If the treatment is administered at the family level, then the family is the unit that should be studied for effectiveness. If it is the neighborhood, then data should be aggregated at that level. In both cases, the individual child is not the proper unit. This basic logic is often not followed. A sufficient number of units needs to be used to assure both that the randomization process can actually have a chance of occurring and that there is sufficient statistical power to detect meaningful differences. While the latter is true for all designs, the requirement for a sufficient number of units to randomize places a special burden on the evaluator. A sample size of three or five units will not ensure that the laws of chance will operate. Since the number of units studied is directly related to cost, this often makes good randomized experiments expensive. In general, however, the randomized design will still be a more efficient estimator of program effects than nonrandomized designs.

(5) *Recognize that generalizability may not be an issue.* Generalizability may not be threatened by the randomized design. Of greater concern is the generalizability of the program under evaluation. Would the program, if adopted, have the same types of clients and personnel administrating the program? If yes, then the problem of generalizability is not as severe. Volunteers for the randomized experiment may be similar to volunteers for the actual program. Finally, the contribution of the randomized experiments to the limits on external validity may seem insignificant in comparison to the problems of generalizing from any study or demonstration to an actually implemented program.

(6) *Be careful of experimental contamination.* The evaluator using a randomized design should be sensitive to the problems of contamination. Contact between clients in the control group and treatment group may result in a demoralized control group or a more

motivated control group (we will get better without their program). In addition, the evaluator needs to be aware of possible contamination caused by third parties. Some agencies may try to provide additional services to the control group in an attempt to "compensate" them for their exclusion from the treatment. If it cannot be assured that the units will not communicate with each other, the evaluator should try to measure the degree of contamination throughout the study period.

(7) *Remember: The simpler the better.* Research designs implemented in the field should be simple compared to multifactorial laboratory designs. The simplest design consists of a treatment and a control group. Evaluation implementation, like program implementation, is a difficult and time-consuming task. The more complicated the design, the higher the probability that it will fail. Does this suggest that evaluation can answer just one question? In a strong causal sense, yes. However, a "black box" or simple input-output design can be avoided. The complexity is not in the impact evaluation design but in the multiple types and sources of data that are included to try to understand program process. Simplicity of design leads to another recommendation.

(8) *Remember also: The stronger the better.* While a significant theoretical or conceptual base (Bickman, 1985) should be maintained, it is recommended that the "kitchen sink" approach be used in program development. Include all reasonable and practical components in the program if it is a new program. The evaluator will have more difficulty in determining the causal chain between the program activities and outcomes, but this may result in a larger effect. If the evaluator leans too heavily toward construct of cause validity, so as to produce a pure and unconfounded independent variable (i.e., the program), he or she will probably produce an ineffective program. Establish the effect first. Then there may be funds available to try to unconfound variables. If the new program fails to produce an effect there is usually not a second chance.

## Quasi-Experiments

When subjects or other units cannot be randomly assigned to treatment and control conditions, the evaluator can fall back on quasi-experiments. Most introductory research texts describe the various designs that fall under the rubric of quasi-experiments. The central principle of all these designs is to eliminate threats to internal validity either by using a variety of comparison or control groups or by collecting data at multiple times from the treatment group. In order to reduce threats to validity, the evaluator needs to understand which threats are *plausible* for a specific evaluation. Different types of designs, that do not share the same type of threat, are often possible.

It is inaccurate to consider quasi-experiments as a set of specific designs. Individual quasi-experiments need to be developed for particular evaluations to eliminate specific alternative explanations or threats to internal validity. However, there are some general approaches to the development of control groups that can serve as guides in this area.

*Control group obtained from other settings.* If it is not possible to assign clients randomly, it may be feasible to use a comparison group composed of other families that are being served in other programs. The goal is to find families similar to the ones served by the family preservation program. Data from these families would then be collected at the same point in time as data from the experimental group. These families may be in other geographic or catchment areas or another unit of one of the referring agencies. The goal is to try to demonstrate that these families are as similar as possible to the ones treated in the intensive home services. The weakness of this design is the probability that these families will not be equivalent to those in the treatment groups and that this lack of initial equivalence will contribute to any differences at follow-up. These initial differences might include severity of the problem, recruitment and selection processes of the referring agency, and neighborhood support systems. The more similar the two groups in selection and assignment, the more viable is this approach.

*Overflow method.* In this procedure, cases are assigned to the treatment when there are openings, but when the treatment program is full the additional referrals are assigned to a control group. When new positions open up again the clients are assigned to the treatment

again. This is not truly a random process because the case flow
be determined by factors that also shape the types of referrals made.
Thus a referring agency may assign more clients with fewer problems at one point in time, see that they are not being served, and
thus assign fewer clients who have more severe problems. Similarly, since the referring agency often knows when a project is full,
"overflow" referrals may consist of families of lower priority for
service. Both patterns of referral would cause the control group to
be composed of individuals with less severe problems than the
treatment group.

*Matching.* A seemingly logical alternative to random assignment
is to match the families in the control group on key characteristics
to the families in the treatment group. This is to be distinguished
from matching pairs of families and then randomly assigning them
to treatment or control groups. In the quasi-experimental matching
procedure, random assignment does not occur. The primary weakness of this method is that it is usually not possible to match on
more than one or two key variables. Moreover, having matched two
groups on these variables, the evaluator is still uncertain whether
they are equivalent on other characteristics—both measured and
unmeasured.

*Time series.* An often viable alternative to random assignment is
the collection of data from a treatment group at many points in time.
This design reduces many threats to internal validity such as
maturation and history. However, this design is not relevant to
family preservation programs because it may require up to 40 time
samples to obtain reliable results. These designs are useful when
the program naturally produces very frequent data on a daily or
weekly basis. Out-of-home placement, a key outcome variable,
does not occur with enough frequency to make a time-series design
feasible.

Quasi-experiments are more difficult to design and analyze than
randomized experiments. Suggestions for specific designs and
analytic approaches can be found in Cook (1983), Cook and Campbell (1979), Kenny (1975), Shadish, Cook, and Houts (1986), and
Trochim (1986). More recent specific examples of how alternative

designs reduce the threats to internal validity can be found in Reynolds and West (1987).

## Statistical Modeling

Statistical modeling is another approach that can be used to deal with problems of internal validity. The evaluator can plan to use either structural equation modeling techniques or econometric techniques (e.g., see Heckman & Holtz, 1987). These are fairly technical approaches that require significant statistical skills as well as some critical assumptions about the data. Compared to randomized experiments these approaches are relatively inefficient in detecting significant program effects. Davis and Bickman (1987) have shown that they require much larger sample sizes to obtain the same level of efficiency as randomized experiments. These procedures also demand highly reliable measures. Typically, multiple indicators of each relevant variable are needed. Finally, there are significant statistical assumptions that need to be made about the data that may be tenuous. If expert advice is available it is certainly recommended that the evaluator anticipate the possible use of these techniques in planning the evaluation.

## Statistical Conclusion Validity

### What Is Statistical Validity?

Are the results statistically significant? In quantitative studies the evaluator will conduct statistical tests to determine if the results of the evaluation were possibly due to chance. If the analysis indicates that the effects could have occurred because of chance, then the evaluator needs to examine the evaluation carefully to determine if it was conceivable that the program actually produced an effect but it was obscured because of a weak design. Statistical conclusion validity is primarily concerned with those threats that might make it appear that there were no statistically significant effects when there were in fact effects. The greater the ability of the evaluation to detect effects that are present, the greater the statistical power of the evaluation.

Statistical conclusion validity is a significant and subtle problem. Many evaluation planners are not sensitive to the degree to which the evaluation may be doomed to failure before the data are collected because of insufficient statistical power to detect a meaningful effect. For example, a well-known study of the effects of police patrols found that the presence of police had no effect on victimization rates. However, it was not noted at that time that the statistical power was so low that if victimization rate had been reduced to zero it still would not have been statistically significant (Schneider & Darcy, 1984). In this case the design was not sensitive and the program may have been falsely branded as a failure when in fact the failure should be laid at the door of the evaluation. Well-informed program staff should critically examine the evaluation for deficiencies of this type. Low statistical power may be identified as the alternative to the unpalatable conclusion that the program was ineffective. Evaluators need to design the evaluation to detect an effect that is judged to be of a meaningful size by the stakeholders. But what constitutes a meaningful effect?

## Effect Sizes

What is a meaningful effect? This question can be restated as, What is the smallest difference that we wish to detect between control and treatment groups? Deciding if the results of an evaluation are meaningful or trivial, even if they are statistically significant, is not easy. The size of the effect that is judged to be meaningful will depend on many factors, including the values of the person making the judgment, the cost-effectiveness of the program, and the purpose of the program. For example, in judging the success of a family preservation program, we need to specify the smallest acceptable difference between treatment and control groups in the number of children who are placed outside of the family. This is not an easy judgment to obtain from stakeholders. Individuals involved in the development, funding, or operation of the program often do not have specific outcomes in mind. As a substitute for trying to coerce this judgment from stakeholders, some general guidelines have been developed to help evaluators estimate effect sizes.

Technically, effect sizes are defined as the proportion of variance accounted for by the treatment or as the difference between treatment and control groups measured in standard deviation units. The purpose of using standard deviation units is to produce a measure that is independent of the metric used in the original dependent measure. Thus we can discuss universal effect sizes regardless of whether we are measuring school grades, days absent, or self-esteem scores. This makes possible the comparison of different studies and of different measures in the same study. Conversion to standard deviation units is obtained by subtracting the mean of the control group from the mean of the treatment group, and then dividing this difference by the pooled or combined standard deviations of the two groups. This calculation is represented by the following formula:

$$\text{Es} = \frac{\overline{X}_T - \overline{X}_C}{\sigma}$$

To judge whether or not an effect size is meaningful, some rules of thumb have been developed. The seminal work in this field has been done by Cohen (1977), who developed suggested labels for effect sizes for social science research (see Table 7.1). As Table 7.1 indicates, a small effect size may be considered to be 20% of a standard deviation between the treatment and control group. In variance terms it indicates that the treatment accounted for only 1% of the change in the dependent variable. This does sound small. A limitation of Cohen's suggestions is that they are not based on a systematic study. Later in this chapter, information based on a very

**Table 7.1** Effect Size Categories Designated by Cohen (1977)

| Effect Size Category | Effect Size | Proportion of Variance |
|---|---|---|
| Small | .20 | .01 |
| Medium | .50 | .06 |
| Large | .80 | .14 |

large number of studies that provide better estimates of average effect sizes will be presented.

It is often difficult to interpret the meaning of effect sizes. Is a small effect of no practical significance? Should we design all evaluations so that they are able to detect only large effects? This would certainly be less expensive, given that, generally, less powerful designs require fewer subjects. Another way of interpreting effect size has been developed by Rosenthal (1984), who provides a procedure for converting effect size to a success rate. For example, a medium effect size according to Cohen is .50 standard deviations, or only 6% of the variance. But this is equivalent to a 24-percentage-point difference between control and treatment groups. Thus a program that accounted for a modest 6% of the variance in placement would represent, for example, raising the percentage of children kept with the family from 38% to 62%, or a 63% improvement in the success rate (24/38). This seems to be a pretty good investment.

**Statistical Power**

But are our evaluations designed to detect small or even medium effect sizes? Statistical power, the probability of finding a statistically significant effect if one is present, is a function of the size of the actual effect, the type of statistics used, the sample size, and the alpha level (usually set at .05). Lipsey (1989) examined a number of research literatures to estimate the statistical power of the studies in those areas. He found that in evaluation research the average statistical power of the studies that had small effect sizes was .14. This means that if a small effect was actually present in these evaluations they would be found only 14% of the time. These evaluations would label programs ineffective 86% of the time even though there really was some effect. For large effects the power was .94, which indicates that large effects would be detected 94% of the time. The figure for medium effect sizes was .58. The generally accepted statistical power level is .80. Thus evaluations were adequate primarily to detect large treatment effects. The results are similar for other social science areas.

Lipsey further examined the power of research studies in 17 meta-analyses, based on 1,380 studies, to try to estimate the "true" effect size of programs in relation to the power of the evaluations to detect these differences. Meta-analysis is a quantitative technique in which a large number of individual studies are aggregated in order to obtain an estimate of effect size for a given research area. Because this procedure has much more power than individual studies, we can have more confidence that meta-analyses will detect an effect if one is present.

Although most of the statistical tests used in each of the individual studies comprised by the meta-analyses showed no effect, most of the meta-analyses showed an overall treatment effect of at least .20 standard deviations. In fact, Lipsey reports that the individual researcher had a .50 probability of making an incorrect statistical conclusion about the treatment effect. Flipping a coin would produce the same findings at much less cost than conducting the evaluation. In 90% of the statistical errors the evaluation concluded that the treatment produced no effect when in fact it probably did have an effect.

## Type I and Type II Errors

In dealing with statistical power the evaluator needs to understand the terms *alpha* and *beta* and the respective type I and type II errors associated with them. The evaluator should be sensitive to

**Table 7.2** Relationship Between Alpha and Beta

| | Actual Effect | |
|---|---|---|
| Conclude Effect Present | Yes | No |
| Yes | 1-beta<br>(power) | alpha<br>(type I error) |
| No | beta<br>(type II error) | 1-alpha |

both of these kinds of errors. Table 7.2 shows the relationship between these terms.

The top of the table indicates whether an actual effect exists. The left side indicates whether the study detected the effect. The upper left corner is 1-beta, or the probability of detecting an effect if one is present (i.e., power). The lower left corner represents a type II error—concluding that there was no effect when there actually was one. The upper right corner is alpha, or the probability of concluding there was an effect when there actually was not one present. This is also known as an alpha or type I error. The bottom right quadrant is 1-alpha or the probability of correctly concluding there was no effect present when there was no real effect.

As noted earlier, in evaluations type II errors appear to be more common than type I errors. Researchers avoid making type I errors often at the cost of increasing type II errors. Most of the studies are good at detecting "large" effects but not good at disclosing small effects. This makes it appear that the programs are ineffective and not worthwhile. Instead of blaming the programs, however, we need to examine the adequacy of the evaluation design more closely.

There are a number of factors that could account for not finding an effect when the program actually caused one. All of these elements affect the statistical power of the design, that is, the ability to detect an effect when it is indeed present. The most visible factor that affects statistical power is the size of the sample. One of the first questions that evaluators usually need to answer is how many subjects are needed. If the number of subjects tested is too small, then the evaluator risks missing a real effect. If the sample selected is larger than needed to detect a meaningful effect, then resources used for data collection and analysis are wasted. The concern for sample size is so salient that Kraemer and Thiemann (1987) have devoted an entire book to this issue. However, improving statistical validity by simply increasing the sample size is often very costly and sometimes not possible. There are other factors that should be considered in designing evaluations so as to improve statistical validity.

## Methods for Improving Statistical Validity

Lipsey indicates that there are four factors that govern statistical power. These are discussed in turn below.

*(1) The statistical test.* The same data can produce different conclusions depending upon the particular statistical test used. Parametric tests, like *t* tests, generally have more power than nonparametric tests like chi-square. Moreover, any statistical procedure that reduces within-group variability (i.e., within the treatment or control group, not between treatment and control groups) will improve the statistical power of the design. Statistical control procedures can be enhanced through the use of such procedures as blocking in analysis of variance. Blocking involves categorizing subjects along a dimension that is related to the outcome measure. The evaluator might want to block children on age if age is, for example, significantly related to running away behavior of children. Statistical power is usually increased when the analyst can reduce the "error" term in the analysis. Other techniques that can reduce error include analysis of covariance, repeated measures designs, and split plot designs. Details concerning these techniques can be found in most graduate-level statistical textbooks.

To optimize the use of these techniques, the evaluator needs to identify those characteristics of the client population that contribute extraneous error to the design, sample the clients along those lines, and conduct the analysis recognizing those factors. For example, a researcher may not want to conduct simple random assignment of children to the treatment and control conditions if age of the child is strongly related to the outcome. The power of the evaluation is usually improved if stratified sampling and assignment are used so that the evaluator can be sure that equivalent numbers of children of different ages are included in both treatment and control groups. Age can then be used as a blocking factor in the statistical analysis. Knowledge of which extraneous factors to include can often be gleaned from the research literature and from the program developers.

*(2) The alpha level.* When conducting a statistical test the researcher usually sets the alpha level, or the probability of rejecting the null hypothesis when it is true. The higher the alpha level, the less likely the researcher will commit a type I error—that is, conclude that there was an effect when there actually was not. The probability of making this error is the alpha level. Alpha levels are usually set at .05 or .01. The former indicates that if the results are significant it is likely that only 5 times out of 100 would this be an erroneous conclusion; the latter simply decreases the odds of making this mistake by requiring the results meet the odds of 1 out of 100. However, the higher the alpha level, the smaller the power of the test.

Most researchers are taught to maintain the alpha level at least at .05. They know that if they identify research results as statistically significant that only reached an alpha of .20 it is unlikely that the study will be accepted for publication. The basic sciences require more assurance that the results from a study are not due to chance. In an evaluation the researcher might want to take a greater risk by using a less stringent alpha level. Table 7.3 shows the various trade-offs of different alpha and beta (recall beta is the probability of making a type II error) levels associated with different sample sizes. To keep both alpha and beta at .05 requires a substantial number of subjects except for very large effect sizes. For example, if both alpha and beta are relaxed to .20, then an effect size of .40

**Table 7.3** Approximate Sample Size Needed to Attain Various Equal
Levels of Alpha and Beta for a Range of Effect Sizes

| Effect Size | Level of Alpha and Beta (alpha = beta) | | | |
|---|---|---|---|---|
| | .20 | .10 | .05 | .01 |
| .10 | 900 | 1715 | 2600 | 4810 |
| .20 | 225 | 430 | 650 | 1200 |
| .30 | 100 | 190 | 290 | 535 |
| .40 | 60 | 110 | 165 | 300 |
| .50 | 35 | 70 | 105 | 195 |
| .60 | 25 | 50 | 75 | 135 |
| .70 | 20 | 35 | 55 | 100 |
| .80 | 15 | 30 | 45 | 75 |
| .90 | 10 | 25 | 35 | 60 |
| 1.00 | 10 | 20 | 30 | 50 |

SOURCE: Lipsey (1989). Copyright Sage Publications, Inc.

would be detected with a sample size of 60 per condition. Maintaining both at high levels of .05 would require 165 subjects per condition, a sample size not found in most family preservation evaluations. Lowering alpha would allow the discovery of more treatments that may be effective. Of course, the risk of this procedure is that programs may be judged effective when in fact they are not. If the evaluation is to assist in making a policy decision concerning the introduction of a very expensive program, then the evaluator needs to balance the cost of possibly implementing an ineffective program with the cost of missing the discovery of an effective one.

Lipsey recommends that when the cost of both types of errors are equal that the alpha and the beta be set equal. As noted earlier, convention usually places alpha at .05. Cohen (1977) recommends that beta be set at .20 (actually power or 1-beta at .80). This implies that alpha (type I) errors are four times more important to avoid than beta (type II) errors. If these two types of errors are to be treated with equal concern, then it could be argued that alpha should be decreased to .20 to match beta or that beta should be increased to .05. The problem with the latter solution is that most studies in the social sciences do not even have a beta of .20, let alone a beta of .05. If both beta and alpha are set at .20, then we can be assured that the probabilities of committing both type I and type II errors are equivalent.

*(3) Sample size.* Sampling error is a significant factor in determining statistical significance. Smaller samples have greater error associated with them, thus increasing the required size of an effect to achieve statistical significance. It should be emphasized that *sample size* refers to the statistical sampling unit. If a single person receives the treatment independently of others, then the individual is the unit of analysis. However, if the unit that is selected and assigned to the treatment or comparison group is the family, then sample size is the number of families and not the number of persons participating in the study. This error most often takes place in educational research when classes are assigned to treatment and control groups and the treatment is delivered to the class as a unit but the investigator uses individual student data in the analysis instead of aggregating the data to the class level.

In family preservation programs it is sometimes difficult to identify the unit of analysis correctly when there is more than one child eligible for the intervention in the family. Averaging the data for the children in the family may not be an appropriate strategy because the behavior of the children may not be independent. For example, as one child improves and requires less attention the other may regress in order to obtain more attention. One way to deal with this problem is to analyze the data separately for multiple-child families. This would provide separate estimates of success for families of different sizes. Another, more limiting, strategy is to restrict the study to families that have only one eligible child. There is no easy solution to this problem, and researchers dealing with families continue to struggle with it. The evaluator at least needs to be sensitive to this issue in analyzing and interpreting the data.

Increasing sample size to improve statistical power seems like an obvious and simple strategy. However, additional subjects are not always available and there is a large cost associated with increasing the size of the sample studied. Not only do additional

**Table 7.4** Approximate Sample Size per Experimental Group Needed to Attain Various Criterion Levels of Power for Range of Effect Sizes at Alpha = .05

| Effect Size | Power Criterion | | |
|---|---|---|---|
| | .80 | .90 | .95 |
| .10 | 1570 | 2100 | 2600 |
| .20 | 395 | 525 | 650 |
| .30 | 175 | 235 | 290 |
| .40 | 100 | 130 | 165 |
| .50 | 65 | 85 | 105 |
| .60 | 45 | 60 | 75 |
| .70 | 35 | 45 | 55 |
| .80 | 25 | 35 | 45 |
| .90 | 20 | 30 | 35 |
| 1.00 | 20 | 25 | 30 |

SOURCE: Lipsey (1989). Copyright Sage Publications, Inc.

subjects need to be recruited, but often this requires adding new sites or prolonging the evaluation so that data from additional clients can be collected. Additional subjects also increase the costs of printing questionnaires or hiring more interviewers, paying more subjects, and preparing and processing data. The evaluator should try to increase statistical power without resorting to increasing the sample size.

As an example of the costs associated with sample size, Lipsey found that the median statistical power for studies he reviewed was .40 (i.e., less than half of the value recommended by Cohen), with an average of 40 subjects in each treatment and control group. This means that the evaluator had less than a 50/50 chance of detecting a real effect. Table 7.4 further emphasizes the costs associated with increasing power by simply increasing the size of the sample. For example, the table indicates that for an effect size of .40 (an average size) and power set at .95, 165 subjects would be required *in each condition* for that effect to be detected. Clearly, alternatives to increasing sample size should be explored.

*(4) Effect size.* The larger the actual size of the effect, the easier it will be to detect. The size of the effect will depend on two factors.

Recall that the definition of effect size is the difference between the treatment and control group divided by the standard deviation. Anything that influences either the size of this difference or the within-group variance will influence the size of the effect. Effect size can be enhanced by increasing the difference between the treatment and control groups and/or decreasing the variability within each group.

The difference between the treatment and control groups will be affected by the *integrity of the treatment*. If the treatment degrades, then the effect size will be reduced by decreasing the potential difference between the two groups. It is important to maintain the strength and integrity of the treatment (Yeaton & Sechrest, 1987) not only for construct validity but for power reasons as well. For example, if a family preservation program includes counseling as one of its program elements, then it is important to ensure that all the clients in the treatment group receive the same level and quality of counseling. If some families fail to attend their sessions regularly (almost a certainty in most programs) or if some clients receive services from experienced and well-qualified counselors while others receive services from poorly trained or new counselors, this will reduce the strength of the treatment.

The lack of consistency in the delivery of the treatment will also reduce the effect size by increasing the within-group variability. There is a tendency in most programs for the treatment to degrade over time. It is easier and less expensive to deliver weak and inconsistent treatments than powerful and consistent ones. It is critical that treatment fidelity be monitored in any comprehensive evaluation. Moreover, the evaluator can help maintain or increase statistical power by suggesting that strong treatments be used, that control groups be guarded against contamination, and that the outcome variable be collected at the time that the treatment is believed to have its maximal effect.

Outcome variables must be valid, sensitive, and accurate to have good statistical power. Selection of measures is an important aspect of planning the evaluation. Certain measures are more sensitive to detecting effects than others. For example, if a program attempts to change a child's self-esteem by five points on a particular scale and the instrument can detect changes only of ten points, it will appear that the program failed. The outcome measures selected must be not only valid but also sensitive to change. Floor and ceiling effects can reduce sensitivity to change. In general, psychometric measures (e.g., standardized achievement tests) are less sensitive to change then criterion-referenced measures (e.g., mastery tests). The evaluator can increase the reliability of the instrument by aggregating across a large number of data points (or measures) at one time, over more points in time, or across more individuals.

Composites of measures are more reliable than single indicators or items. In general, continuous measures can detect differences better than categorical measures can. As an indication of how reliability can influence effect size, Lipsey indicates that a reliability of .50 can reduce effect size by about 70% when compared with a perfectly reliable measure. The evaluator may need to conduct pilot studies to examine measurement issues if there is not adequate research using the candidate instruments on the target population.

While this chapter does not deal directly with particular outcome measures, it is recommended that the data collected include more than just the specified objectives of the family preservation project. The evaluator also needs to examine if there are any unintended negative or positive side effects that the program planners did not anticipate.

Variability in data collection can also affect the within-group variance. Since most evaluations are not conducted in laboratories, it is difficult, if not impossible, to control or eliminate all extraneous influences. The recording of case data by different workers is a difficult source of variability to overcome, but good training can decrease such variability. For example, if data are collected from a child under noisy or stressful conditions it is bound to influence the reliability of those data. Evaluations conducted with families with little or no formal education will usually require interviews instead of self-administered questionnaires to assure that the data are collected in a uniform fashion and that the respondent understands the questions. This, of course, increases the cost of the evaluation.

Finally, the heterogeneity of the sample studied increases variability. Some of this variability can be reduced by more narrowly defining eligibility for participation. Some programs reduce eligibility by legal status of the child, number of past placements, severity of abuse, and the like. In addition, the evaluator may need to resort to some of the statistical techniques described earlier. These strategies include simple blocking on variables that relate to the dependent variable in conducting the data analysis. For example, it would be good practice to block on gender in most studies because the behavior of boys is often very different from that of girls, especially when antisocial behavior is an outcome variable. A blocking variable that correlates .75 with the dependent variable will increase effect size by as much as 50%. For correlations below .50 there is little to gain from blocking, but higher correlations can have a large impact on the effect size. This is not an insignificant multiplier, especially when the effect size is small. Analysis of covariance and repeated measure designs can accomplish similar gains.

In general, effect size poses the most difficulty for the evaluation planner. Alpha level, sample size, and the statistical model can easily be established, but estimating effect size is much more difficult. As noted above, it depends on the following factors:

- the strength and fidelity of the treatment
- the sensitivity of the dependent variables
- the extraneous variability in the dependent measures
- the actual size of the difference between the treatment and control groups

Lipsey suggests three ways to estimate effect size.

**Estimating Effect Size**

The evaluator can take an actuarial approach to estimating effect size. If there is sufficient research in the family preservation area, the evaluator can use the previous studies to compute the effect sizes found in these evaluations. Although effect size is not reported in most studies, the techniques used in meta-analysis can be used to compute effect sizes from a variety of statistics (see Rosenthal, 1984, for procedures). Existing meta-analytic studies can be very useful in predicting effect sizes. There are hundreds of such studies already published. Using these studies it is possible to have some confidence about what effect size can be expected. For example, if a meta-analytic study indicated that the average effect size was .50, with the lower quartile being .25, then the evaluator may want to establish the power of the design to detect a difference as small as .25 standard deviations if the evaluation is to detect any effect larger than the 25th percentile of the studies in that meta-analysis.

There do not appear to be any meta-analytic studies of family preservation evaluations, but there are studies in the counseling and psychotherapy literature that might prove helpful. Lipsey found that the average effect size for 89 meta-analyses in these areas was .44. This can be interpreted to indicate that, on the average, the treatment group exceeded the control group by almost a half standard deviation. Psychological or behavioral interventions produced an effect size of .56, while educational interventions had an average of .37 standard deviations. In contrast to Cohen's (1977) rule of thumb for labeling effect sizes, these data can be used to categorize effect sizes empirically. Table 7.5 shows the relative ratings of effect sizes based on the 89 meta-analyses. Lipsey labeled an effect small if it was in the lower 25th percentile, medium if it was in the middle 50th percentile, and large if it was in the upper 25th percentile. Using this table an evaluator who wanted to detect a medium effect size for using a psychological intervention should be sure that the design has sufficient statistical power to produce statistically significant results for an effect size of .36 standard deviations or more.

A second approach to estimating effect sizes is to translate or convert existing data statistically into effect sizes. Lipsey describes how to compute effect sizes from studies that present normed data, success rates, or proportion of variance. These unstandardized

**Table 7.5** Small, Medium, and Large Positive Effect Size Ranges
Based on Meta-Analysis of Treatment Effectiveness Research

| Range | Values of Effect Sizes | Midpoint |
|---|---|---|
| All treatments | | |
| small | .00-.23 | .12 |
| medium | .24-.65 | .44 |
| large | .66-1.20+ | .93 |
| Psychological/behavioral treatments | | |
| small | .00-.35 | .18 |
| medium | .36-.74 | .55 |
| large | .75-1.20+ | .98 |
| Educational treatments | | |
| small | .00-.22 | .11 |
| medium | .23-.49 | .36 |
| large | .50-1.20+ | .85 |

SOURCE: Lipsey (1989). Copyright Sage Publications, Inc.

formats (not divided by the standard deviation) are usually easier for people to understand. For example, if a family preservation evaluation found that the children in the control group stayed with their families 45% of the time and the treatment group 55% of the time (a 22% improvement in the success rate), this difference in success rate would translate to an effect size of .20 standard deviations. Interestingly, this 22% increase in success (10/45) is equivalent to accounting for only about 1% of variance in the outcome. Different indices can influence the perception of the strength of an effect. In this example percentage of variance, and even effect size, appears small compared to a difference in percentages.

Another approach to estimating effect sizes is to set a criterion for success. This is a pragmatic approach that attempts to answer the question about the practical significance of the evaluation outcome. In order to use a criterion approach the evaluator needs to find examples or comparisons of a naturally occurring effect that is judged to be of a meaningful size. Assume that the evaluator is interested in judging the effect of a family preservation program on juvenile delinquency recidivism but was not sure how much of an effect should be expected. A naturally occurring comparison could be sought. Lipsey constructed such a comparison between minor offenders and major offenders on frequency of arrest six months after the initial police contact. This approach assumes that the effect size between these two groups would be of practical significance. If an intervention program "made" the recidivism rates of serious offenders appear similar to those of minor offenders, then this could be considered a program that produced a significant effect. Lipsey found an effect size of .26 between these two categories of offenders, which is equivalent to a correlation of .13 or a differential success rate of 44% versus 56%. Other examples of this approach include the following:

- computing effect sizes for an additional year of schooling on achievement scores
- comparing eligible versus ineligible clients (severity)
- comparing "normal" subjects and target population
- maturational differences

There are other approaches to determining the smallest practical effect size, including comparing the outcome with the costs of the program. Interpretation of this information will be a matter of judgment, but it is sometimes helpful to examine the cost per unit outcome to determine if the program is worthwhile. It is important that the evaluator confirm the minimal effect size estimates with program personnel and other stakeholders. These estimates may be difficult for them to interpret, so the evaluator should attempt to place these effect sizes in context by supplying comparable effect sizes for other programs or criteria groups. Most often the evaluator expects a larger effect than experience dictates. As a result, the evaluation design is not sensitive to smaller effects and the program appears to be a failure.

**Estimating Statistical Power**

The most comprehensive source for estimating statistical power is Cohen's (1977) seminal work. This book contains a wealth of tables that are extremely useful for evaluators. Lipsey's book provides a simplified approach that is based on just two group comparisons (i.e., treatment versus control). Instead of tables, Lipsey uses charts. To use these charts the investigator first decides which three of the four factors (sample size, alpha, effect size, statistical power) that influence statistical power will be fixed and then finds the fourth one. Separate figures are provided for different alpha levels. In some cases effect size, alpha, and sample size are fixed and the evaluator needs to determine the power of the design. In planning, the evaluator may set power, effect size, and alpha and want to know what size sample will be needed. In these charts statistical power is depicted on the vertical axis and the sample size on the horizontal axis. Each curve on the chart represents a different effect size. The charts present a generic effect size that can be computed from different statistical procedures (e.g., analysis of variance, chi-square). The evaluator simply specifies the sample size (for each group, not the total $n$; use harmonic mean for unequal $n$s) and the expected or actually determined effect size to obtain the power of the evaluation. Lipsey provides details on how to calculate effect size from the results of different statistical procedures.

Many evaluations fail before the first datum is collected. Too often, the design does not have sufficient statistical power to detect the effects of the program. Evaluators have generally not been sensitive to the combination of small effect sizes and weak designs. This combination is the formula for failure, failure that often has mistakenly been attributed to inadequate programs rather than faulty evaluations. Moreover, when evaluators have been aware of power concerns they have mistakenly believed that sample size is the only solution. It is hoped that this chapter has demonstrated that an increase in sample size should be considered only after the sensitivity of the measures, delivery of treatment, statistical analysis, and alpha level have been thoroughly explored. If planning indicates that power may not be sufficient, then the evaluator faces the choice of not conducting the evaluation, using a qualitative technique, or simply informing the clients of the risk. Whichever is chosen, if the power issues are thoroughly and openly discussed the decision will be an informed one, not one glossed over in the haste to get the program and the evaluation started.

## *Conclusion*

This chapter has reviewed design requirements that evaluators should be sensitive to in planning a family preservation evaluation. Evaluation design attempts to deal with threats to four types of conclusions about the evaluation:

(1) Are the findings statistically significant?
(2) Are the effects due to the program and not to extraneous factors?
(3) Why did the program influence relevant outcomes?
(4) Can the results be generalized?

This chapter focused on the first two concerns: statistical power and internal validity. Both of these terms were reviewed and specific suggestions were provided to increase the validity of the design. In particular, family preservation program evaluators need to pay special attention to the statistical power of the evaluation. Methods for increasing statistical power include the following:

- lowering the alpha level
- increasing the sample size
- improving the consistency and strength of the treatment
- increasing the sensitivity of the measures
- using advanced statistical procedures

It is suggested that internal validity is best dealt with by using randomized designs. A number of suggestions are provided on how best to implement a randomized field experiment. Alternatives to random assignment include quasi-experiments and statistical modeling. Both of these procedures have disadvantages associated with them that argue for the use of randomized experiments. If family preservation programs are efficacious, then this should be demonstrated to potential funders and others who would adopt these services. A well-designed outcome study is a rational way to accomplish this.

## References

Bickman, L. (1985). Randomized field experiments in education: Implementation lessons. In R. F. Boruch & W. Wothke (Eds.), Randomization and field experimentation [Special issue]. *New Directions for Program Evaluation, 28.*

Bickman, L. (Ed.). (1987). *Using program theory in evaluation.* San Francisco: Jossey-Bass.

Boruch, R. F., McSweeny, A. J., & Soderstrom, E. J. (1978). Bibliography: Illustrative randomized field experiments. *Evaluation Quarterly, 4,* 655-695.

Boruch, R. F., & Wothke, W. (Eds.). (1985). Randomization and field experimentation [Special issue]. *New Directions for Program Evaluation, 28.*

Campbell, D. T., & Stanley, J. C. (1966). *Experimental and quasi-experimental designs for research.* Chicago: Rand McNally.

Cohen, J. (1977). *Statistical power analysis for the behavioral sciences.* New York: Academic Press.

Cook, T. D. (1983). Quasi-experimentation: Its ontology, epistemology, and methodology. In G. Morgan (Ed.), *Beyond method: Strategies for social research.* (pp. 74-94). Beverly Hills, CA: Sage.

Cook, T. D., & Campbell, D. T. (1979). *Quasi-experimentation: Design and analysis issues for field settings.* Chicago: Rand McNally.

Davis, K., & Bickman, L. (1987). *The no free lunch school of design: Can selection problems be solved without randomized experiments?* Unpublished manuscript.

Guba, E. G. (1987). Naturalistic evaluation. In Evaluation practice in review [Special issue]. *New Directions for Program Evaluation, 30.*

Heckman, J., & Holtz, V. J. (1987). Do we need experimental data to evaluate the impact of manpower training on earnings? *Evaluation Review, 11*(4), 395-427.

Kenny, D. A. (1975). A quasi-experimental approach to assessing treatment effects to the nonequivalent control group design. *Psychological Bulletin, 82,* 345-362.

Kraemer, H. C., & Thiemann, S. (1987). *How many subjects? Statistical power analysis in research.* Newbury Park, CA: Sage.

Lipsey, M. W. (1989). *Design sensitivity: Statistical power for experimental research.* Newbury Park, CA: Sage.

Reynolds, K. D., & West, S. G. (1987). A multiplist strategy for strengthening nonequivalent control group designs. *Evaluation Review, 11,* 691-714.

Rosenthal, R. (1984). *Meta-analytic procedures for social research.* Beverly Hills, CA: Sage.

Schneider, A. L., & Darcy, R. E. (1984). Policy implications of using significant tests in evaluation research. *Evaluation Review, 8,* 573-582.

Shadish, W. R., Jr., Cook, T. D., & Houts, A. C. (1986). Quasi-experimentation in a critical multiplist mode. In W. M. K. Trochim (Ed.), *Advances in quasi-experimental design and analysis.* San Francisco: Jossey-Bass.

Trochim, W. M. K. (Ed.). (1986). *Advances in quasi-experimental design and analysis.* San Francisco: Jossey-Bass.

Yeaton, W. H., & Sechrest, L. (1987). No-difference research. *Evaluation Practice in Review, 34,* 67-82.

# About the Authors

**Leonard Bickman,** Ph.D., a leader in applied social psychology and program evaluation, is director of the Program Evaluation Laboratory of Vanderbilt University. He is also Director of the Vanderbilt Institute for Public Policy Studies Center for Mental Health Policy. He has served as Director of the Westinghouse Evaluation Institute. He teaches courses in program evaluation and applied research methods, and his areas of expertise include mental health policy, education policy, and program evaluation.

**Leonard Feldman**, M.A., is completing work on his Ph.D. in the Graduate School of Social Work, Rutgers University. He is Chief of the Bureau of Research, Evaluation and Quality Assurance within the New Jersey Division of Youth and Family Services, that state's public child welfare agency. He is currently conducting an evaluation study of the division's Family Preservation Program initiative in four New Jersey counties. He was an active member of the Conference Planning Committee for the American Public Welfare Association-sponsored National Conference on Research, Demonstration, and Evaluation in Human Services in 1989.

**Mark Fraser**, Ph.D., is an Associate Professor and Director of the Ph. D. Program at the Graduate School of Social Work, University of Utah. He received his B.A. from DePauw University, his M.S.W. from Denver University, and his Ph.D. from the University of Washington in Seattle. His experience in youth services includes YMCA work, managing a group home, and providing a variety of child, parent, and family services as a school social worker. For approximately ten years, he has worked with Homebuilders, assisting with various research and evaluation projects. He is the author of numerous articles, chapters, monographs, reports, and manuals focusing on families and children.

**Kristine E. Nelson**, D.S.W., is an Associate Professor at the University of Iowa School of Social Work. She has been associated with the School's National Resource Center on Family Based Services since 1980, serving as Principal Investigator on four federally funded studies of intensive family services and of child neglect. Her practice experience includes public welfare and social services, and she has published in the *Journal of Social Service Research, Social Service Review, Children and Youth Services Review, Journal of Sociology and Social Welfare*, and *Catalyst*. An article she has written on family-based services for juvenile offenders is forthcoming in *Children and Youth Services Review*.

**Carol L. Pearson**, Ph.D., is currently employed as the Director of Research at the Montgomery County, Maryland, Department of Social Services. Prior to this, she was the Chief of Research and Evaluation for the Maryland Social Services Administration in Baltimore. She received her Ph.D. in social welfare from the University of Maryland at Baltimore and her A.M. in social work from the University of Chicago.

**Michele Rivest**, M.P.A., is currently directing a special study examining the independent cross system implementation of family preservation services in North Carolina. She also works with the North Carolina Child Advocacy Institute as Vice President for Programs. She has worked in the child welfare field for the past fifteen years, developing children's services and policies at the national and state levels. She has published extensively in the field, and has recently completed work on two reports—*The Children's Budget* and *The State of the Child*—for the state of North Carolina. She is the former Director of the Children's Program at the National Conference of State Legislatures. She holds a master's degree in public administration from the University of Colorado.

**Ying-Ying T. Yuan**, Ph.D., is Vice President of Walter R. McDonald & Associates, Inc., a human services management consulting and information systems development firm. She received her doctorate degree from the Department of Social Relations, Harvard University. For the past ten years she has focused her attention on the assessment of human services systems in the United States. She has conducted evaluations of programs serving families and their children at the federal, state, and local levels. Currently she is Principal Investigator of an evaluation of eight intensive in-home services demonstration projects funded by the California Office of Child Abuse Prevention. She is also assisting the Connecticut Department of Children and Youth Services and the American Indian Law Center in their evaluations of family preservation programs. She is a Board Member of the National Association of Family Based Services.